RICHARD DUNSTON LIMITED
SHIPBUILDERS OF THORNE AND HESSLE
A PICTORIAL HISTORY

Opposite: T.508 *(22-09-44) TID 99 (65ft x 17ft x 8ft), one of the 159 TID steam tugs built by Dunstons during the Second World War, seen on the canal at Thorne, shortly after completion, with a group of Sea Cadets on board.*

RICHARD DUNSTON LIMITED
SHIPBUILDERS OF THORNE AND HESSLE

A Pictorial History

MIKE TAYLOR

WHARNCLIFFE BOOKS

First published in Great Britain in 2009 by
Wharncliffe Local History
an imprint of
Pen and Sword Books Limited,
47 Church Street, Barnsley,
South Yorkshire. S70 2AS

ISBN: 9781845630942

A CIP catalogue record of this book is available from the
British Library.

Pen and Sword Books Ltd

Printed in the United Kingdom by CPI

Pen & Sword Books Ltd incorporates the imprints of
Pen & Sword Aviation, Pen & Sword Maritime,
Pen & Sword Military, Wharncliffe Local History, Pen & Sword Select,
Pen & Sword Military Classics and Leo Cooper.

For a complete list of Pen & Sword titles please contact:
PEN & SWORD BOOKS LIMITED
47 Church Street, Barnsley, South Yorkshire, S70 2AS, England.
E-mail: enquiries@pen-and-sword.co.uk
Website: www.pen-and-sword.co.uk

Opposite: The two 61½ ft x 15½ ft (Sheffield size) Humber keels, T.1 Southcliffe *and* T.114 Shirecliffe, *both completed in 1923, lie moored at Hull the 1930s with sails furled and bearing their original masts and leeboards.*

Contents

Acknowledgements

With the encouragement and practical help of Arthur Credland (Keeper) and his assistant Sue Cape, I have used items from Hull Maritime Museum's collection of Dunston material. Frank Dallas, George Trevethick and Mr J P Glasby have also given valuable assistance. Additionally, I am indebted to the owners of several pictures for making them available to me.

A Dunston billhead of the late nineteenth century, showing the Thorne shipyard and its dry dock alongside a fancifully widened Stainforth & Keadby Canal with several wooden craft under construction and one under sail. The labelled etching shows, from left to right, sail loft, rope walk, Dunston offices, smiths' shop, saw mill and mast maker. Behind the buildings lie piles of timber.

Introduction

IN 1858, RICHARD DUNSTON sold his boatyard at Torksey, near Lincoln, on the Fossdyke and established another yard 12 miles up the Stainforth & Keadby Canal from the River Trent, at Thorne. The Dunston view of the company's early history was published in the mid-1950s within *Almost a Century of Shipbuilding* and its story may be continued from that book:

> ... The new shipyard was kept busy constructing wooden vessels of up to about 80 tons carrying capacity for use in the Humber and its tributaries. In those days of sail, rigging paid such an important part in the ...

construction of the vessel that it was customary for small shipyards to be completely self-contained making sails, ropes and running gear. The Thorne shipyard ropery developed into quite a small independent industry which supplied coir, hemp, manilla and even cotton ropes to the surrounding country.

The ships' chandlers of Hull and Grimsby also found this shipyard their principal source of supply for ships' blocks, masts, spars, boat hooks, boat oars, sails and covers. In those days it was the proud boast of this inland shipyard that they supplied everything that a sailing ship required from the keel of the vessel to the truck that was fitted on the mast head.

On the old wooden hulls, repairs made an important part of the shipyard trade, and the production of new ships was a matter not to be undertaken lightly. When a third new ship was launched in a year, this was recorded as quite an event, contrasting greatly against the Company's best output in recent years of 108 ships in one year.

The timber used for the construction of these craft was grown locally, brought into the yard and sawn by hand, and it was some considerable time before the conversion of timber was done by power saw. Ships were mostly clinker built, as it was only in the later years of wooden shipbuilding that carvel form of construction became popular.

Towards the end of the 19th century the sizes and types of new barges began to standardise into what became known as the "Sheffield Keel," and a square rigged barge of 90/100 tons, and the somewhat larger "Humber Sloops."

In 1902, the founder, Richard Dunston, died and control of the shipyard fell to the lot of the son, Thomas Dunston. No notable change appears to have taken place in the shipyard until Thomas Dunston died in 1910, and at the young age of 20, the present Chairman, the grandson of the founder, assumed control. It

did not take many years for him to appreciate that the days of the wooden barge were rapidly coming to an end and sweeping changes in the shipyard were soon made by the erection of buildings and plant designed for the construction of iron and steel ships. Such must have been the enthusiasm at this time for "new ideas" that only one further wooden vessel was constructed by the Company, and a new era of progress commenced. Each year brought an increase in the size and variety of craft constructed, and the demand developed from being local to international. In the passage of years it soon became apparent that this more widespread demand was calling for ships which could be constructed by the shipyard, but which could not pass through the canal to the sea. Canal locks would not pass vessels with a beam of more than 21 feet, and after straining this capacity to the limit, the present Chairman, in 1932, acquired the shipyard of Henry Scarr, Ltd., of Hessle-on-Humber, where vessels with no dimensional limitations could be launched directly into the River Humber, thus enabling the Company to develop the construction of larger ships. It is interesting to note that a number of wooden men-of-war were once constructed at Hessle, and records show that the first, named the *Humber*, an 80-gun ship, was built in 1693.

The Hessle yard was completely remodelled. Two of its nine berths were covered in and the remaining seven berths and slipways were reconditioned. The skilled personnel was developed, as in the Thorne yard, to be able to complete not only the hull of the vessel, but the joinery and fittings, and installation of the main and auxiliary machinery and electrical equipment. Tugs of up to 1,200 h.p. were soon being constructed, coasters up to 600 tons D.W., and lighters up to 1,200 tons D.W.

This formed a great advance of the maximum size of those vessels constructed at the Thorne yard, which had been 700 b.h.p. tugs, 300-ton D.W. coasters and 300-ton D.W. lighters.

The year 1942 saw a further notable change. The many advantages of electric welding had been realised by the Company for some considerable time, and welding had become part of the normal processing, but a policy decision was then made to lay aside a portion of the yard specially for the construction of all-welded ships which were at that date somewhat of a novelty. In this way the shipyard became the pioneers in this country of the construction by bulk production methods of all-welded ships of the smaller type. During the war they built on production lines for the Admiralty, no less than 159 all-welded steel tugs of one type. On these war-time tugs, by careful production control, the completed ships, including the installation of steam machinery and auxiliaries, were produced at a rate which permitted vessels to leave the shipyard at six-day intervals. Many other types of craft were built during the war for the Admiralty, and for Foreign Governments after the cessation of hostilities.

The first all-welded trawler to be built in this country came from this yard, and the great majority of tugs ordered for the Thames since 1936 have come from either the Thorne or Hessle yards.

Progress in modernising and equipping of the yards continues, and under the more specialised methods which are now arising, the control has become more and more technical, and checking of quality of production more complex. It is a vastly different picture from the peaceful shipyard of the founder, and in these days of impersonal combines, it is of considerable interest to note that the progress to be made in the immediate future will still be directed by the direct line of the founder, his great-grandson, the present Managing Director.

Welded Craft

1943-1953—551 Vessels of all Types.

In 1933 it was found that all-welded fabricated steel counters for Thames tugs were equal to and lower in cost than the cast steel type previously incorporated. When it was seen that the welded counter was able to withstand the arduous working conditions encountered on the River Thames, it was obvious that here was a form of construction which should be developed. Progress in welding at both the Thorne and Hessle yards has continued steadily ever since.

From the welding of small assemblies to the completely welded vessel has, of necessity, taken many years, principally due to the cautious attitude of both the shipbuilder and the shipowner. It was not until 1942, when the Admiralty placed orders for 12-220 i.h.p. steam tugs that the first all-welded vessel was constructed. These craft proved to be most successful, and subsequently orders were completed for a total of 159 steam tugs, 36 diesel tugs, and 36 400-ton D.W. coasters.

In 1948 two all-welded 570 b.h.p. diesel tugs for operation on the River Thames were built. These have been most successful and subsequently a further two sister ships were ordered. It is interesting to note that these were the first all-welded tugs to be built for operation on the Thames.

Since 1949 five all-welded drifter-trawlers, the first of their kind, have been constructed for operation in home waters. These vessels were so successful that contracts for three all-welded Trawlers for the North Sea were received.

In 1946 it was decided that the London swim barge was an ideal type for construction by welding and both yards were laid out for the rapid production of barges, and by the end of 1953 218 had been produced. Where numbers are ordered an appreciable saving can usually be shown ; for example, a Thames barge of 220-tons D.W. is cheaper to construct than a riveted barge of the same dimensions. Apart from first cost there are other features which command attention, such as reduced repair bills; the welded structure has greater strength and resistance to damage which tends to remain localized, and when too severe to be faired up can be cut out and a new complete section welded into position. Quicker construction is obtained due to reduced handling and the fewer number of trades involved. Large pre-fabricated sections are constructed away from the berth, and as a result of this the time taken to assemble and launch is very much less than that required for a riveted vessel. The reduction in the weight of the light ship gives greater carrying capacity for a given displacement and a smooth hull is obtained which reduces water resistance.

The following vessels completed during the past few years give an indication of the progress of the all-welded vessel, 40 300-ton D.W. river tankers, one 500-ton D.W. river tanker, one 300-ton D.W. tanker, four 125 ft. B.P. hopper barges, seven motor lighters, and one floating dock.

RE-ERECTION WORK.

At the Thorne and Hessle Yards space has been laid out for the accurate fabrication and erection of tugs, barges and other vessels required to be shipped overseas in either units or plates and sections and over a long period of years a special technique has been developed to facilitate erection abroad.

As cargo-carrying on Britain's rivers and canals started to lose out to road and rail transport in the 1960s, the number of orders for Humber and Thames inland waterway freight craft diminished and Dunstons began to concentrate on tug-building. More orders were also taken for vessels for overseas owners, as well as for fishing vessels, workboats and craft for the Admiralty and Ministry of Defence.

Dunstons were one of the largest shipbuilders to be left un-nationalised in the late 1960s as the British shipbuilding industry began its decline. This left them without artificial financial-aid devices such as the Regional Employment Premium, which 90% of their more northerly nationalised competitors received. Nonetheless, as the 'Cod War' began the demise of the British fishing industry, thus killing off another outlet, they stayed at the forefront of developments in tug propulsion, begun earlier by involvement with Kort units, and continued through those of Voith-Schneider, Aquamaster and others. They built some tractor tugs (powered by units positioned amidships rather than at the stern) and made it abundantly clear to prospective customers that they also built coasters, small tankers etc, indeed anything within the size limitations of their building berths.

In the early 1980s, the Hessle site had a workforce of 280 manual workers and 70 staff responsible for marketing, technical, financial and drawing office services. Thorne had eighty manual workers and fifteen staff.

Shipbuilding ended at Thorne in 1984, the yard closed in 1987 and the site was cleared by 1993. It is now covered by a private housing estate. Hessle closed in 1994, the site has not been redeveloped. Dunston Ship Repairs, established in 1993, continues the family name to this day, operating in Hull's William Wright Dock.

A total of 1358 vessels were built at Thorne and 636 vessels at Hessle after 1932, when the yard came under Dunston ownership.

Photographs, dating from the late nineteenth century to the early twenty-first, constitute almost all the illustrations used in this book. Each illustration is credited separately, apart from those taken by me or selected from my collection, which are left uncredited. Generally, pictures of craft have been arranged throughout the book in chronological order of their completion. Yard records available for pre-1930 craft are incomplete, but for those vessels built since that time, a standard caption format, introduced with the first picture in the book, has been adopted. This gives the yard number (prefix T. indicates Thorne, S. (Scarr) indicates Hessle, changed to H. in 1975, followed by date of completion, name of the vessel, dimensions to the nearest ½ft (length between perpendiculars x beam x draught), description of vessel (sometimes as given in the yard list), the manufacturer of its engine and horsepower (if I have been able to discover these), the first owner and, finally, details of the actual picture used, with its date and any other relevant points of interest.

Emphasis has been placed on craft built to work on inland waterways, mainly those built to carry commercial cargoes. Ship-handling tugs, ocean-going ships, fishing vessels and Royal Navy craft have received less detailed attention.

The following abbreviations have been used:

A&CNC Aire & Calder Navigation Co.
APCM Associated Portland Cement Manufacturers
BOCM British Oil & Cake Mills
BTC British Transport Commission (1953-1962)
BWB British Waterways Board, later British Waterways (1963-2007)
D&IWE Docks & Inland Waterways Executive (1948-1953)
MoD Ministry of Defence
S&SYNC Sheffield & South Yorkshire Navigation Co.
SPV Self-Propelled Vessel

Also, 'ihp' has been used for indicated horsepower and 'bhp' for brake horsepower. The latter is derived from practical testing of the vessel, whilst ihp is a theoretical calculated value often used for steam engines and is usually about twenty per cent higher than that for bhp.

Chapter One

Before 1932

PRIOR TO 1932, DUNSTONS' operation was concentrated at their Thorne shipyard and this chapter deals solely with activities there. Absence of complete yard lists for the period means that, in this chapter, the aforementioned standard caption format cannot be adopted in every case.

By 1900, Dunstons had changed from producing clinker-built (overlapping planks) wooden vessels to carvel-built (abutting planks) craft. They began to concentrate on shipbuilding and steadily increased their rate of production from an average of one and a half vessels a year between 1858 and 1914. Their first steel vessel was built in 1917 and the yard had changed over completely to this material by the mid-1920s as demand for wooden craft declined. Between 1920 and 1925, W Bleasdale & Co, major traders to Sheffield, had nine steel sailing keels built at Thorne, plus four that were mortgaged to them out of seven built for the S&SYNC. In the period 1925 to 1929, Harkers, who had not yet begun to build their own tanker barges, had ten such vessels produced, some fitted with motors. Many craft were Sheffield-size (61½ft x 15½ft). The largest vessel built at the yard before 1932 was the 100ft x 20ft steamer Trent.

A view of wooden craft at Dunstons' Thorne yard, dating from about 1900. The vessel in the foreground is clinker-built, whilst the one further down the canal (Bleasdales' Brincliffe), is carvel-built. Alan Oliver Collection

Built by Dunstons in 1898, Annie Maud *was one of four wooden carvel-built keels owned by Robinson Brothers, the Rotherham millers, and is shown in the 1930s as its sail is being lowered (to be followed by the mast) to negotiate Thorne railway bridge whilst en route for Hull. After discharging its cargo of coal there, grain would be collected from the docks for the return voyage.*
(Humber Keel & Sloop Preservation Society)

The carvel-built keel Mayday, *owned by Thos Hanley & Sons, the Doncaster millers, was launched at Dunstons in 1900 and is shown light, with mainsail raised, ready to lock out into the Trent at Keadby and voyage to Hull to load imported grain for its owners.* Mayday's *leeboard and cog boat would probably also have been built by Dunstons.*

The carvel-built wooden keel Guidance *was built in 1905 for William Henry Schofield by Worfolks of Stainforth, a couple of miles up the canal from Thorne. Like many wooden sailing craft built at various S&SYN boatyards, it was brought to Dunstons to be rigged with mast and sails and is shown heading down the Stainforth & Keadby Canal section of the S&SYN in the 1940s. The ropery was one of the first parts of the yard to be dispensed with in 1911, the company choosing to rely on external suppliers from that time on.*

Guidance *is shown later in the 1940s at Waddingtons' Swinton yard being extensively refurbished, making it good for another 40 years work on the S&SYN.*

The carvel-built wooden keel Furley's Else *was built for Furley & Co by Dunstons and completed in 1914. It is shown in the then traditional pose for a new sailing vessel, outside the boatyard with the skipper's family aboard and sails fully raised.* Alan Oliver Collection

Selby oil mills had five 95½ft x 17½ft x 7½ft 220 ton capacity steel lighters built by Dunstons in 1921 to join their large fleet of tug-hauled dumb craft carrying imported seeds from Hull docks to their premises beside the river Ouse. T.98 Selby Argo *was one of these and is shown, with its name truncated, at Selby in 1971 flanked by two of BOCM's modern SPVs, after the owners had moved away from tug-hauled dumb barges.* Tony Lewery

T.116 *Furley & Co's steel Sheffield-size keel* Gar*, completed in 1924, sailing on the S&SYN near Doncaster in 1936.*

T.107 Dovecliffe, *completed in 1923 for Bleasdales, discharging grain at the silo in the northern corner of Sheffield basin in the early 1950s, having been motorised by a 21bhp Lister engine in 1945.* BWB

In the cluttered southern corner of Sheffield basin, T.122 Lightcliffe, *complete for Bleasdales in 1924 and motorised with a 21bhp Lister in 1937, is discharging cases of ferroalloys after being taker over by the BTC in 1957 fo Bleasdales' non-payment o tolls.* BWB

BWB's Sheffield-size T.114 Shirecliffe *and* T.106 Wharncliffe, *both completed in 1923 for Bleasdales, loading oversic at Goole after being motorised by 21bhp Lister engines in 1945 and 1953 respectively.* BWB

T.118 *The Sheffield-size* Highcliffe, *completed in 1924, discharging at Knostrop depot, Leeds in the late 1950s, after, like* Lightcliffe, *being taken over by the BTC from Bleasdales. The vessel had been motorised in 1943 by installation of a 21bhp Lister engine.* BWB

Early in 1925, Richard Dunston wrote letters to possible customers seeking work for his men on building or repairing wooden boats. This reply from the TNC's Frank Rayner was typical of the responses he received. The last new wooden vessel, Constance, *was completed in 1925 for an Owston Ferry carrier.*

Trent Navigation Company.

GENERAL MANAGER'S OFFICE.

TELEPHONE 2881 (PTE. BRANCH EX.)
TELEGRAMS: "TRAFFIC, NOTTINGHAM.

Wilford Street,
Nottingham.

Reference R.N.

PLEASE ADDRESS REPLY TO GENERAL MANAGER. 9th January, 1925.

Dear Mr.Dunston,

I have received your letter of yesterday and am sorry to hear that your wood shipbuilding department is so slack. I am sorry that I have nothing I can put in your way just now.

Yours faithfully,

F Rayner

Richard Dunston Esqre.,
Messrs. R. Dunston Limited.,
The Shipyard,
THORNE,
nr.Doncaster.

T.128 *(30-06-25)* Beecliff *a Sheffield-size vessel built for the S&SYNC and mortgaged to Bleasdales, fitted with a 21bhp Lister engine in 1937, lies moore outside Rotherham old dep on the S&SYN in 1960, shortly before a new depot was built in the town.* T.118, Highcliffe *(see above) is also visible.*
Graham Hague

Another Sheffield-size kee built in 1925 to be mortgaged to Bleasdales u T.132 Whitcliffe, *shown i the 1950s passing a small sailing vessel on the Top Level of the S&SYN as it approaches Sheffield basin with a cargo of wheat.*

Yet another Sheffield-size keel built in 1925 for the S&SYNC and mortgaged to Bleasdales was T.133 Ferncliffe, *shown waiting to collect grain from the silo in Hull's King George Dock in the 1950s. The vessel was fitted with a 21bhp Lister engine, also mortgaged to them by the S&SYNC in 1937.* Associated British Ports

Most sailing vessels built at Thorne were rigged as 'square-sailed' Humber Keels, but a few Humber Sloops, differing from keels only in their rigging and shapes of sails, were produced. T.131, *the sloop* Annie H *was built in 1925 for J W Handson and is shown at Dunstons' fitting out berth below Thorne railway bridge shortly before being handed over to its owner.* Alan Oliver Collection

T.136 *(02-10-25)* Michael *(61½ft x 15½ft x 7½ ft) an 80 ton capacity motor tank barge fitted with a 56bhp Ellwe engine, built for Harkers, is shown nearing completion on the canal at Thorne.*

T.137 *(26-11-25)* Tony *(74ft x 14ft x 5½ ft), a 55 ton capacity motor tank barge fitted with a 60bhp Widdop diesel engine, built for Harkers, is shown in 1932 moored in Liverpool docks.*

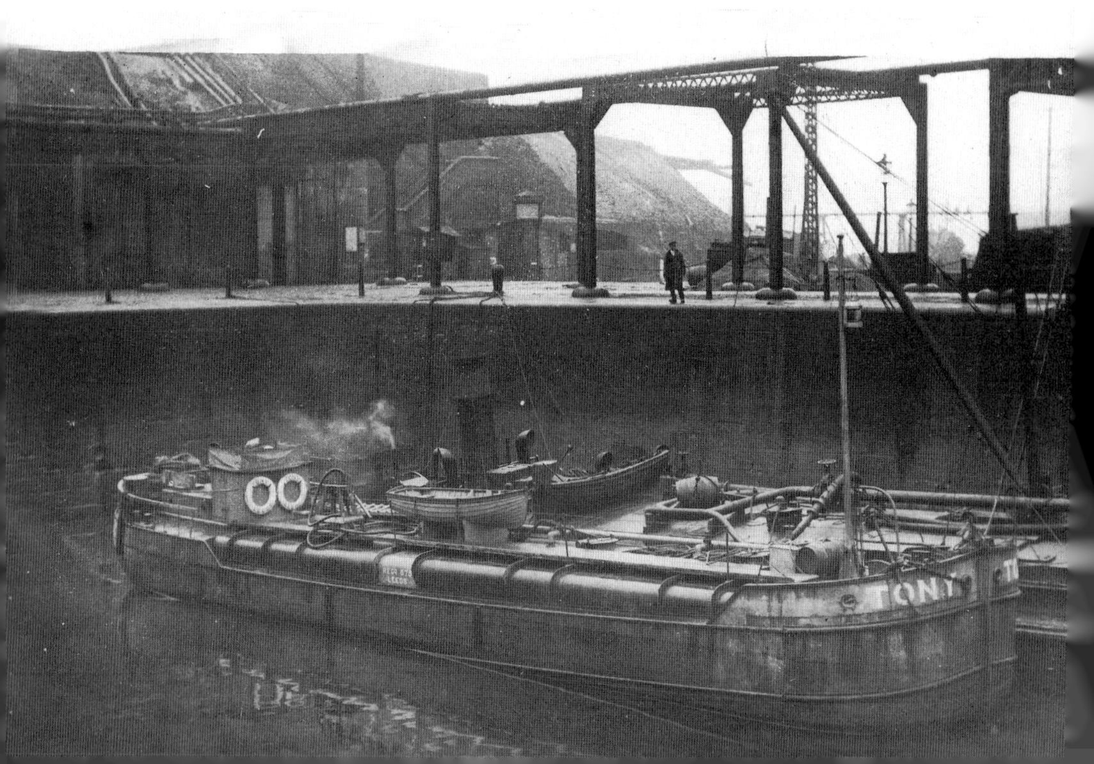

T.142 *(07-06-26)* Salvager *A (72ft x 16½ft x 7½ft), a sloop, was built for A Leggott of Owston Ferry. A Swedish engine was installed in 1933 and the vessel is shown shortly afterwards as passengers board the vessel on the Trent at Gainsborough.*
Les Reid Collection

T.153 *(14-11-28)* Rosa H *(82ft x 15½ft x 7½ft), a 110 ton capacity dumb tank barge built for Harkers and, at the time, under the control of their Gloucester office, stuck under Worcester's main road bridge over the Severn in floods during January 1936.*

T.164 *(02-10-29)* A Victory *(76½ft x 17½ft x 7½ft) a motor barge built for James Barraclough & Co waiting below Newark town lock, bound for Nottingham with wire in 1982, when owned by Gainsborough Shipping. The original 90bhp 'foreign' engine had been replaced by a 77bhp Lister Blackstone engine in 1957 and the vessel had been lengthened to 109?ft in 1970.*

T.170 *(16-04-30)* Drake *(82ft x 15½ft x 7½ft), a dumb tank barge built for James W Cook & Co (at the same time as their motor tank barge* T.171 Dauntless*) shown on acceptance trials in the Humber, off Hull's Victoria pier. Both vessels were lost due to enemy action in January 1942.*

T.178 (12-09-32) Danum (611/2 ft x 151/2 ft x 71/2 ft), a 'Sheffield lighter' built for Hanleys of Doncaster. Initially, the vessel was worked under sail until motorised by installation of a 60bhp Widdop single cylinder engine in 1944 and is seen entering Rotherham lock, bound for a nearby mill, in the 1960s.

T.186 (09-10-31) Gainsborough Trader (70ft x 161/2 ft x 71/2 ft), a 110bhp Widdop-engined motor barge built for Furley & Co. This was the Co's first newbuilt SPV and is shown on trials on the River Trent.

T.187 *(12-12-31)* Trent *(100ft x 20ft x 8ft), a steamer built for the Grimsby Packet Co, and at this time, the largest vessel launched at Thorne. Converted to diesel power by installation of a 150bhp Gardner engine in the 1950s, the vessel is shown delivering an imported cargo of tinned fruit on the Trent at Beckingham, near Gainsborough, in the early 1970s.*

Chapter Two

1932-1939

BY THE EARLY 1930s, Dunstons no longer made sails and had ceased to rig craft at Thorne, though they continued for a few more years as mastmakers and blockmakers. They acquired Henry Scarr's yard at Hessle in 1932 and continued building, now exclusively in steel, at both Thorne and Hessle, though the Hessle yard traded under the Scarr name until 1961. In addition to both dry cargo craft and tanker barges for local waterways, considerable numbers of lighterage tugs and lighters were built for work on the Thames. Welding was gradually introduced to replace riveted joints during the 1930s, initially for only parts of vessels.

The Kort nozzle, consisting basically of a fixed tubular structure around the propeller of a tug, was invented in 1932 to combat bank erosion on rivers and canals by an open-screw vessel's wash. Dunstons built their first Kort-nozzled tug, *Ness Point*, in 1936.

During this period, craft up to 150ft in length (overall) were built at Hessle and up to 90ft at Thorne. In 1937, eight refuelling launches were built at Thorne; the first of many orders from overseas.

T.194 *(28-11-33)* Arc *(62ft x 14½ft x 5ft), a steel motor barge built for Leeds Corporation Electricity Department, was fitted with a Widdop engine and designed to carry coal and tow dumb craft (the towing hook is visible behind the helmsman). Coal from loading staithes on the A&CN was brought up to the new Kirkstall power station on the Leeds & Liverpool Canal and the vessel is seen on a loop of that canal constructed near the power station to facilitate deliveries.*

S.356 *(??-??-33)* Chartners *(55ft x 15ft x 7ft), a 150ihp single screw-steam tug built for the River Lighterage Co seen at work on the Thames in 1948 proceeding upstream from Teddington lock, helping the first Bantam tug to be built on its trials with a loaded lighter. In pre-war days,* Chartners *often towed coal barges up to Staines.*

T.203 *(11-12-33)* No 40 *(75ft x 20ft x 9?ft), a lighter for Ranks, seen in 2001 at Mexborough on the S&SYN, loaded with imported fluorspar for Rotherham when owned by Waddingtons, being push-towed by their motor barge* Northern King. Mike Brown

T.205 (14-12-33) Celerity *(61½ft x 15½ft x 6½ft), a steel dumb barge, built for James Wilby, the Pontefract coal merchant, is seen, still dumb, in 1980 when owned by Waddingtons of Swinton. The vessel is being hauled by rope into Sprotbrough lock on the S&SYN, laden with coal for Doncaster power station.*

S.361 (13-01-34) Rapidity *(75½ft x 15ft x 7ft), a steel dumb barge built for James Wilby Ltd. o carry coal to York from the West Riding of Yorkshire. The vessel, now motorised, is shown iere in 1957 shortly after penning out into the River Ouse at Selby.*

S.372 *(16-12-35)* Aid *(36½ft x 9ft x 5ft), a 'motor and utility launch' built for the River Ouse (Yorks) Catchment Board and shown here moored above Long Sandall lock in 1951, with the 'busboat' in tow.*

T.179 *(19-02-36)* Daybreak *(61½ft x 15½ft x 7½ft), another 'Sheffield size lighter' was ordered by Hanleys at the same time as* Danum *(see page 25). Both vessels, with masts raised and sails furled are shown in the late 1930s moored, loaded at Doncaster wharf with their owners' mill just visible to the left of the view.*

T.255 *(22-04-36)* R 56 *(75ft x 20ft x 9½ft), a 200-ton capacity dumb lighter was built for Ranks of Hull and is shown, after receiving a 'snatch' from a passing tug, drifting into the entrance lock to King George Dock, Hull in 1981 when ownership had passed to Gillyott & Scott.*

S.374 *(27-04-36)* Kittiwake *(81ft x 14½ft x 7½ft), a 'motor petrol barge' powered by a 120bhp Allen engine, was built for James W.Cook & Co. and was itself towed down the East Coast to London in 1939. The vessel, now* Kittiwake C, *is shown towing another tanker down the Thames in the early 1940s delivering petrol, piped from Avonmouth to Walton depot, down to central London wharves during the Second World War.*

Kittiwake C, *after its return to Humber waterways, tows a dumb barge into Bulholme lock on the A&CN in the early 1960s. Both craft would be carrying petroleum liquids to Leeds.* BWB

T.175 *(20-06-36)* Burcroft *(92ft x 19ft x 9ft), a dumb barge built for Hudson, Ward & Co, the Goole millers, was motorised with a 95bhp Gardner engine in 1958 and is shown in 1994, when owned by Holgates, fitted with a 120bhp replacement engine, discharging steel at Rawmarsh Road wharf, Rotherham, with a similarly-loaded lighter in mid-canal.*

S.377 *(02-07-36)* W.M.C. No 10 *(68ft x 17½ft x 7½ft), a dumb barge built for Hull's Waterloo Mills Cake Co. which, after a spell as O 32, became* Ouse *and was fitted with a 62bhp Lister Blackstone engine in 1960 when owned by T F Wood & Co of York. The vessel was motorised in the early 1960s and is shown shortly afterwards discharging clay using its mast and derrick at Thwaite Mills, on the A&CN near Leeds.*

S.379 *(06-08-36)* Spark *(62ft x 14½ft x 5ft), a motor coal barge built for Leeds Corporation Electricity Department to service Kirkstall power station, heads up the Leeds & Liverpool Canal loaded with coal. Since its towline is taut,* Spark *will almost certainly be towing a dumb, coal-laden vessel.* Yorkshire Evening Press

Spark *is shown, after becoming surplus to requirements at Kirkstall, loading coal ex-lorry a*
Mexborough for delivery to the new power station at Doncaster in the late 1950s. BWB

(17-11-36) Staincliffe *(60ft x 15½ft x 7½ft), was one of five motor barges built for the S&SYNC*
and fitted with 21bhp Lister engines. Two of these were mortgaged to Bleasdales (T.385
Rawcliffe *was the other one). The vessel is shown waiting to tranship a cargo in King Georg*
Dock, Hull in the 1950s as its captain poses with a mug of tea.

Staincliffe *is the inner vessel of the pair of inland waterway craft transhipping a cargo from a sea-going vessel in King George Dock, Hull during the 1950s, when owned by BWB.* Associated British Ports

S.388 *(05-04-37)* Isleworth Lion *($65\frac{1}{2}$ft x 16ft x $8\frac{1}{2}$ft), one of the earliest motor tugs to be produced by Dunstons, was built for the Lion Wharf Co. with a 300bhp Widdop diesel engine, and is shown travelling light on the Thames in the late 1930s.*

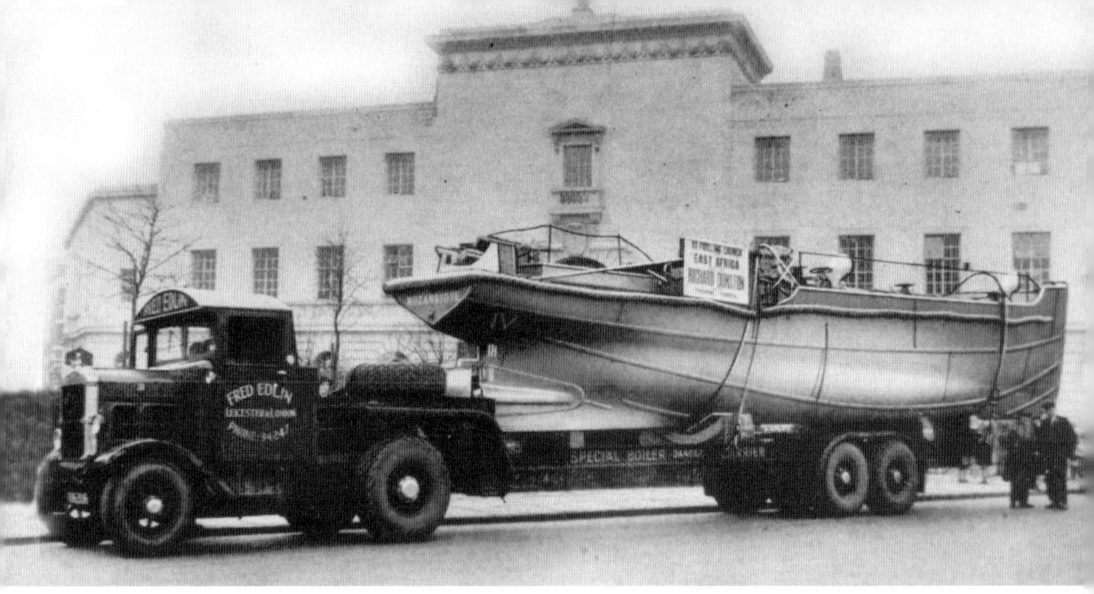

T.296 *(30-04-37)* Mona-Mozambique *(46ft x 10ft x 5ft), a 'refuelling launch' was one of eight built for the Anglo-Saxon Co, one of Dunstons' first overseas customers. The vessel is shown being delivered by road transport to London docks prior to carriage to East Africa.*

T.289 *(06-06-37)* Ness Point *(71ft x 18ft x 9ft), a twin screw, coal-fired steam tug of 360ihp built for the LNER, is shown on the stocks at Thorne with its fixed Kort nozzles (see page 27) clearly visible.* Hull Maritime Museum

.302 (14-07-37) Hanley's Pride *($61\frac{1}{2}$ft x $15\frac{1}{2}$ft x $7\frac{1}{2}$ft), a motor towing barge fitted with a 00bhp Crossley engine, built for the Doncaster millers is shown on its Humber trials.*

pre-Second World War aerial view of the Thames, with ships, tugs and nearly 150 lighters isible above Tower Bridge. This was a scene towards which Dunstons increasingly began to ontribute both tugs and lighters. Seventy-eight Thames lighters were built at Thorne before 1940.

S.397 *(31-07-38)* Cullamix *(76ft x 20ft x* $10\frac{1}{2}$*ft), a 700bhp motor tug, built for the Associatio of Portland Cement Manufacturers (APCM) and here posed on a publicity card in front o Tower Bridge, as barges hauled by a steam tug head up the Thames.* Cullamix *towed man thousands of lighter loads of cement from lower Thames factories to several waterside builders merchants as far upriver as Isleworth, until laid up in the 1970s.*

T.329 *(09-09-38)* Riccall *and* T.126 *(06-05-25)* Attercliffe, *both Sheffield-size, built for Furle & Co and W Bleasdale & Co respectively, are shown waiting to load in Hull's King Georg Dock in 1958. The former vessel was built as an SPV fitted with a 30bhp Lister engine, whils the latter was built by the S&SYNC as a sailing keel, mortgaged to Bleasdales and fitted wit a 21bhp Lister engine in 1937, also purchased under mortgage from the S&SYN.*

S.396 *(28-09-38)* Hurricane *(75ft x 20ft x 10½ft), a 600bhp diesel tug built for James W Cook Ltd is shown on trials when new. A frame to support the canvas 'dodger' and shield the helmsman from the elements may be seen.*

With a more modern conventional wheelhouse fitted, Hurricane *comes down the Thames with lighters in tow when owned by Braithwaite & Dean in 1982. Each of the four lighters shown had earlier delivered 200 tons of maize to Wandsworth and at least two of them were Dunstons-built at Thorne.*

Burnitt 7.1, T.326 (17-08-38) Skell *(61½ftx 15½ ft x 7½ft), a motor barge fitted with a 40bh Ellwe engine, one of three built at the time for Furley & Co is shown transhipping a cargo c newsprint in Goole's West Dock during the 1960s.* Norman Burnitt

T.332 *(15-11-38)* Mobilitie *(61½ft x 15½ft x 7½ft), a motor tank barge fitted with a 50bh Crossley Brothers' engine, built to the order of the Medway Oil & Storage Co for work on th S&SYN, is shown in Teddington lock cut on the Thames in the 1940s. Like* Kittiwake C *o page xx, the tanker had been brought south from the Humber to deliver petrol piped fro Avonmouth to Walton-on-Thames to a wharf below Wandsworth Bridge during the Secon World War.*

T.333 *(21-12-38)* Tenacitie *(61½ft x 15½ft x 7½ft), an identical sister ship of* Mobilitie *is shown moored outside the petrol depot at Walton-on-Thames in the early 1940s where it was also involved in the wartime petrol traffic.*

S.402 *(06-05-39)* Mimo *(61ft x 15½ft x 7½ft), the first newbuilding SPV for the fleet of Richard Hodgson & Sons, the Beverley tanners, was fitted with a 70bhp Swedish engine. The vessel passed to Hudson Ward, the Goole millers, in 1943 and is shown on the Trent at Girton quarry staithe in 1984 when owned by Alan Sellers.*
John Noble Collection

The completed Bluebird *on the canal at Thorne. A second* Bluebird (T.1114) *was built for Lord Riverdale in 1963.*

T.336, *(15-06-39)* Bluebird *(48ft x 11ft), a motor yacht built for and to the design of Lord Riverdale of Sheffield, was a rare pleasure craft to be built by Dunstons. The completed frame is shown.*

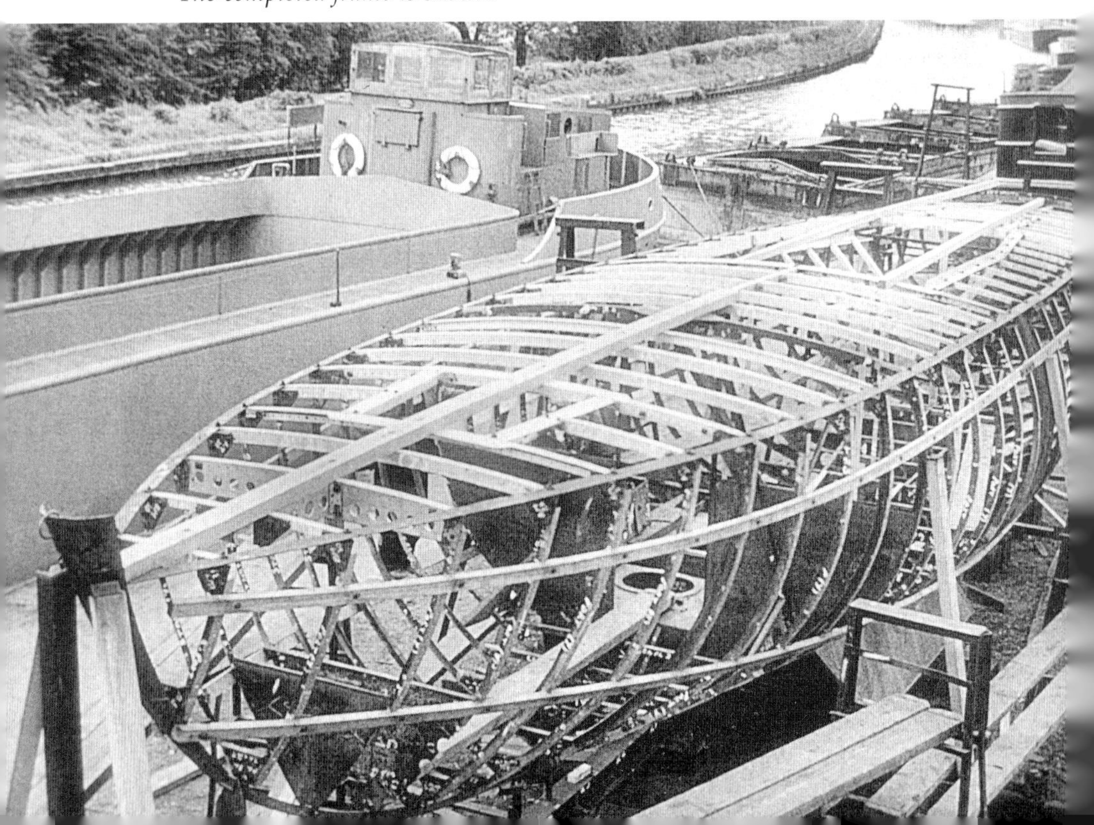

Chapter Three

The 1940s

FOR THE FIRST HALF OF THE DECADE, building of inland waterway craft took second place to the war effort. Most notable was the company's involvement in the design, testing and production of TID tugs, 159 of which were built by the company. Other tugs, colliers, 'Chant' tankers and VIC 'puffers' were also built for the Admiralty or Ministry of Shipping as a mixture of dumb, steam-powered and diesel-powered craft emerged from the two yards. The company had built part-welded Thames tugs in the 1930s and found them entirely satisfactory, so they moved over to 100% welding with the TIDs and many subsequent vessels, becomimg a leader in the introduction of welding into British shipbuilding.

After 1945, a large number of all-welded Thames lighters were produced at both Thorne and Hessle along with Thames tugs and craft for the Humber waterways. Vessels for overseas owners had been built before the Second World War and orders were placed for more foreign owners such as a 36-strong fleet of all-welded steam tugs, at Thorne, for work in Burma and for forty all-welded 300 ton capacity self-propelled inland waterway tankers, at Hessle, for the French government, after yards in their own country had been bombed.

T.349 *(30-06-40)* Vista *(69ft x 18ft x 9ft), a motor tug built for Vokins & Co, shown in 1954 preparing to cast off its timber-laden lighters and nudge them into the cut linking the Thames with the Grand Union Canal for lightermen to manhandle them up to the BTC's Brentford wharf.*

An aerial view showing lighters moored at Brentford depot on the Grand Union Canal in 1980, after BWB had taken it over. Some transhipment of cargoes to narrowboats was undertaken here until the 1970s. APCM had a wharf also serviced by lighters just off the top of the picture.

T.357 *(16-12-40)* Thomas H *($61\frac{1}{2}$ ft x $15\frac{1}{2}$ ft x $7\frac{1}{2}$ft), after conversion to a workboat, is shown heading up the Ouse beneath Cawood Swing bridge in 1984.*

T.356 *(16-12-40)* Richard *(61½ft x 15½ft x 7½ft), a dumb barge was built for Hodgsons of Beverley and launched on the same day as its sister ship* T.357 Thomas. *Shortage of engines meant that the craft were operated dumb until 30bhp Lister engines were fitted in 1943.* Richard *is shown in the late 1940s leaving the Trent for the S&SYN at Keadby lock prior to collecting a cargo of coal for its owners from Hatfield colliery.* Les Hill

T.353 *(31-01-41)* C.447 *(145ft x 34ft x 10ft), an oversize dumb tank lighter too large to leave Thorne by water, was one of three sister vessels built for the Admiralty. After assembly, it was painted red on its port side and green to starboard, then its plates were numbered in white paint before the vessel was dismantled to be shipped overseas for reassembly at its destination.*

This panoramic view of Dunstons' yard, looking east, dates from the early 1940s and shows craft under construction on the building berths to the right adjacent to the canal. One of three oversize tank lighters T.350, T.351 or T.353, is visible on its construction site to the left, well away from the water.
Frank Dallas Collection

T.367 *(14-07-41)* Hegaro *(61ft x $15\frac{1}{2}$f x 8ft), another dumb vessel for the fleet of F Hodgson & Sons that was eventually fitted with a 30bhp Lister engine. The vessel is shown positioned to load opencast coal from lorries at Wakefield in the 1950s.*

T.377 *(25-03-43)* Pinklake *(71½ ft x 20½ ft x 11ft), another single screw steam tug, this one fitted with a 465shp Platt & Son engine, built for the River Lighterage Co. hauling two Dunston-built lighters on the River Thames. Notice the flimsy protection afforded to the helmsman by the open wheelhouse and its canvas 'dodger'.*

T.397 *(12-01-43)* Fred Bray *(61½ ft x 14½ ft x 6½ ft), an eighty ton capacity dumb barge built for the Leeds Industrial Co-operative Society to be hauled to/from collieries on the A&CN by the company's tugs and towing barges and discharged at Leeds. The vessel is shown waiting to be loaded at Parkhill Colliery staithe on the A&CN's Wakefield branch in the 1960s.*

T.393 *(30-07-43)* Empire Laird *(140ft x 21½ ft x 10ft), a 'self-trimming diesel collier' built for the Admiralty and deployed to Bristol owners for delivering coal to Portishead and Gloucester power stations is shown nearing completion at the yard. Its single propeller was powered by a 275bhp Crossley engine, An outline of delivery problems caused by the breadth of the vessel is given later in the book.*

Tugs in Dock (TID)

One of Dunstons' major achievements was the wartime design, testing and production of TID (Tugs in Dock) tugs. These were assembled by welders, several of whom were female, joining together eight units manufactured by non-shipbuilding companies. These units, each weighing less than six tons and with maximum dimensions of 10ft x 17ft x 13ft, were readily able to be lorried to Thorne. For well over a year after the first TID was completed in February 1943, a finished TID left Thorne every five days.

The units of a TID tug arranged in final assembly order, viewed from across the canal at Thorne, together with some of the Tom Puddings in which their engines and boilers were stored.

TID tugs moored on the canal at Thorne for fitting out and installation of their 220ihp steam engines.

T.508 *(22-06-44)* TID 99 *(65ft x 17ft x 8ft) passes Hull docks prior to handover. Thorne built 152 TIDs, the first 90 were coal-fired, this one was oil-fired.*

T.427 *(15-11-43)* TID 27 *(65ft x 17ft x 8ft), one of the coal-fired TIDs, on wartime duties off Falmouth, with its wheelhouse consisting of a canvas 'dodger' evident.*

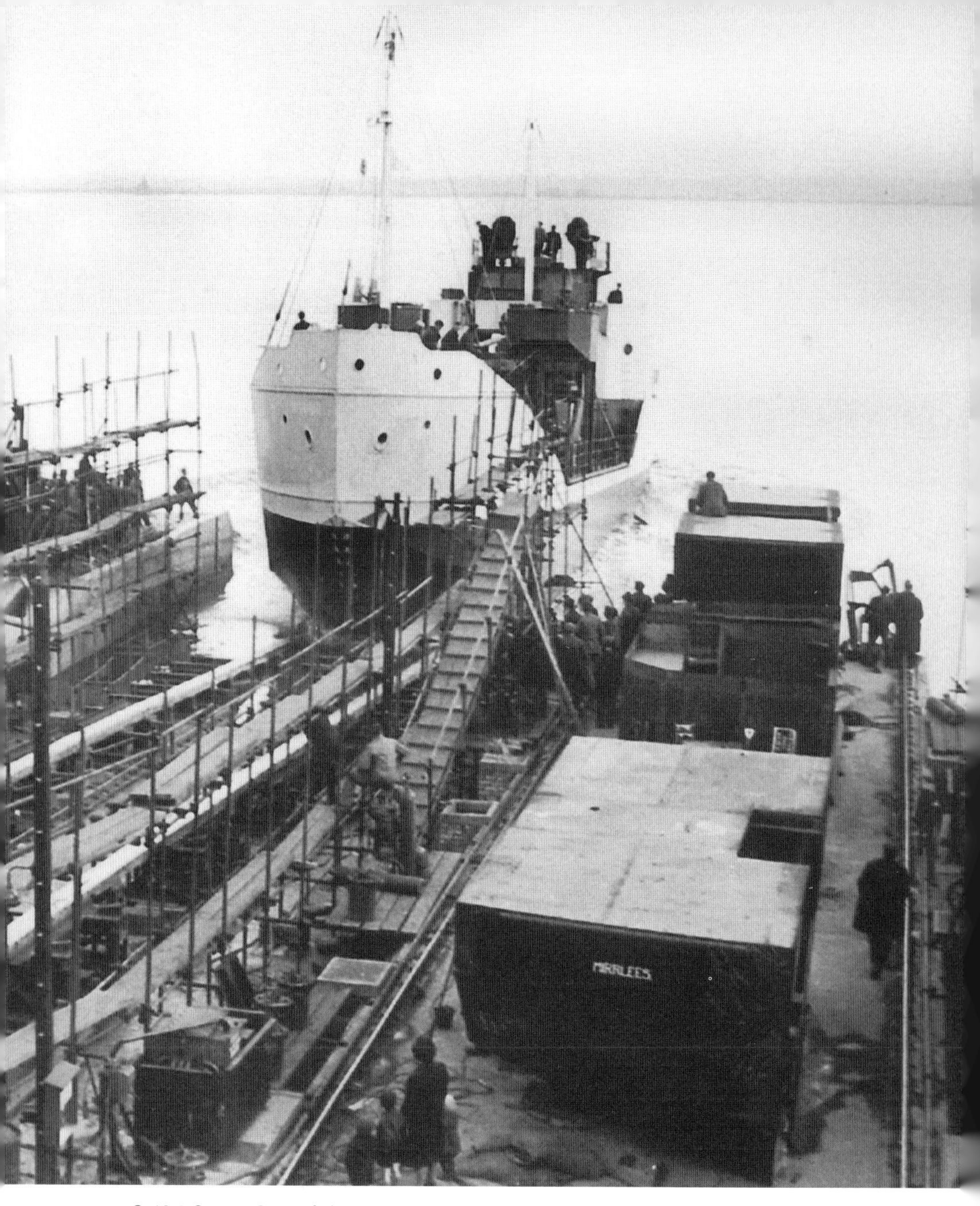

S.435-S.446 *One of the twelve all-welded 'Chant' motor tankers (141ft x 26½ft x 13½ft) fitted with a 220bhp Crossley Brothers' engine, built for the Ministry of Shipping between February and July 1944, being launched at Hessle. These craft were capable of being run aground on French beaches to deliver fuel oil, petrol or fresh water.* Hull Maritime Museum

T.389 *(04-11-42)* VIC 23 *(67ft x 18½ ft x 9½ ft) a coal-fired steam 'puffer' (a reference to the engine noise made by the direct exhaust of the condenser-less steam engines fitted to earlier flat-bottomed craft developed for use on Scottish waterways and coastal services, on which their designs were based), built to supply naval requirements in the Second World War. (VIC stands for Victualling Inshore Craft). The vessel, photographed on trials off Hull, was fitted with a 113bhp Sissons steam engine and a Cochran boiler.*

T.457 (22-09-44) VIC 45 *(67ft x 18½ ft x 9½ ft), a diesel steel 'puffer', one of 36 built by Dunstons (27 steam-powered, 9 diesel-driven) for the Ministry of Shipping, shown passing Hull's Riverside Quay when new. A Crossley Brothers' 150bhp engine was installed at the time.* Hull Maritime Museum

T.521 *(09-06-44)* Ruth *(78ft x $16\frac{1}{2}$ft x 8ft). A 200 ton capacity dumb barge built for James Hargreaves & Sons was one of the few exclusively inland waterway vessels built by Dunstons during the war years. It is shown at Thorne, a few hours after being launched.*

S.478 *(24-11-45)* TID 170 *(65ft x 17ft x 8ft), an oil-fired vessel, one of seven TIDs built at Hessle and one of the 69 oil-fired TIDs of the 159 built by Dunstons. The total of 182 TIDs was completed with twenty-three constructed at Sunderland by William Pickersgill & Co.* TID 170 *is shown in Hull's Alexandra Dock with funnel lowered and its open screw (i.e. Kort nozzle-less) propeller visible, ready to be lifted aboard the former liberty ship* Samtweed *by the floating steam crane for carriage to the far east as deck cargo.*

T.573 *(07-09-45)* Neo *(61ft x 15½ft x 8ft) a diesel coal barge built to join Hodgsons' fleet which had acquired* Richard *and* Thomas H *in 1940,* Quebo *and* Hegaro *in 1941 and* Dritan *17 days after* Neo. *The illustration shows Neo powered by a 40bhp Gardner engine, discharging a cargo at Waddingtons' newly-built wharf at Eastwood, near Rotherham in the early 1960s*

T.579 *(05-07-45)* Silverdot II *(41ft x 12ft x 6½ft), a 120bhp National Gas & Oil diesel powered, single-screw Thames towing launch built for Silvertown Services, handlers of water traffic around Tate & Lyle's busy sugar import wharf on the north bank of Woolwich Reach.*

T.643/4/5/6 (27-11-45) steel flats (50ft x 11ft x 3½ft), built for the S&SYNC, one of which was converted to a 'busboat' by placing the passenger compartment of a Rotherham Corporation omnibus into its cargo space. The dumb vessel is shown moored at Thorne in 1961 and also appeared on page xx when being towed by Aid. Geoff Warnes

The 'busboat' in use for an inspection party to view parts of the S&SYN in 1948. The raised instrument being demonstrated is a man-blown foghorn.

One of the four flats T.643-T.646 *is shown in 1972, loaded with apparatus, being used in the demolition of Conisbrough lock on the S&SYN. This could even have been the former 'busboat'.*
Norman Burnitt

T.580-T.615, *thirty-six 'B' class Irrawaddy twin-screw all-welded diesel tugs, each fitted with two 100bhp Crossley engines, were completed between 25-05-45 and 20-06-46 on Admiralty orders for Burma's Irrawaddy Flotilla Co. The section of Thorne yard nearest the canal lock was set aside for construction of welded vessels and three of these tugs are shown at various stages of construction.*

T.608 *(29-03-46)* B.39 *(72ft x 16ft x 6ft) was one of the 'B' class tugs built for work on Burma's Irrawaddy river and is shown here, prior to being exported, towing a barge on the Humber.*

S.485 *(18-01-46)* Teviot *(86ft x 21ft x 9ft), built for the River Lighterage Co. was one of the first of many all-welded Thames lighters to be built by Dunstons and the 200 ton plus capacity vessel, is shown on the slip at Hessle.*
Hull Maritime Museum

S462 (20-04-46) Mavis *(140ft x 26ft x 11ft), a single screw 465bhp diesel coaster built for the General Steam Navigation Co and one of the earliest 'short sea ships', made regular voyages on the inland waterways of Europe to cities such as Cologne in the late 1940s and 1950s.*

S.599 *(20-11-48)* Brent Brook *(68ft x 19½ft x 9½ft), a 520bhp diesel tug built for the Thames-based River Lighterage Co is featured in this advertisement for Russell Newbery & Co's engines. This was the first all-welded tug referred to in the Dunston history.*

RN
RUSSELL NEWBERY
RN
RUSSELL NEWBERY
"BRENT BROOK"
One of 4 All-Welded Single-Screw Diesel Tugs. Length B.P. 68′ 0″. Breadth Moulded 19′ 6″. Depth Moulded 9′ 6″. Machinery : 520 B.H.P.
Also illustrated are the 2 Auxiliary sets supplied by RUSSELL NEWBERY & CO. LTD., of Dagenham, specialists in diesel-driven marine auxiliary equipment up to 120 H.P. including emergency fire pumps, as used by the leading Ship-owners at home and abroad.

T.673 *and* T.674 *(21-06-47)* Frances *and* Noel *(62ft x 15½ ft x 6½ ft), two 100 ton capacity dumb coal barges built for James Hargreaves & Sons, the Leeds-based coal merchants, lie ready to be launched at Thorne.*

One of S.511-550 *(between 20-08-47 and 07-06-48)* Jacquelin *(127½ft x 16½ft x 10ft) one of forty 300 ton capacity 104bhp motor tankers built from all-welded prefabricated units for the French government because their own yards were still out of action following the Second World War. They were to be used on the inland waterways of northern France where the photograph was taken.*

T.696 (12-04-48) Lapwing C *(81ft x $15\frac{1}{2}$ft x $7\frac{1}{2}$ft), a 'power tank barge' fitted with a 170bhp Ruston & Hornsby engine, built for James W.Cook & Co and used for delivering petrol to Trent and A&C terminals. The vessel was lengthened by 30ft in 1956. It capsized over Whitton Sands with the loss of three lives in 1961, and is shown on the A&CN, after repairs, heading towards the new A1 road bridge at Ferrybridge in the late 1960s.* John Noble Collection

T.698 *(25-10-48)* Revenge *(65ft x $17\frac{1}{2}$ ft x $8\frac{1}{2}$ ft), a 330bhp Crossley-engined single-screw Thames diesel tug was built for Wm.Cory & Sons and is shown here on the Thames shortly after delivery.*

Revenge *was bought in 1983 by BWB, who were attempting to maintain traditional Thames lighterage on the river after several companies had ceased to trade. It is shown with a replacement wheelhouse towing Dunston-built lighters up Bow Creek in 1983.*

T.769 *(28-07-49)* Dunham *(74½ ft x 14½ ft x 7ft) a welded motor barge fitted with a 30bhp Lister engine built for Furley & Co is shown here in Lofthouse Basin on the A&CN's Wakefield Branch in the 1960s.*

Chapter Four

The 1950s

THIS WAS DUNSTONS' MOST ACTIVE decade in terms of the number of craft built. Thorne built 254 vessels, including twenty-three tugs, 156 lighters/dumb barges and thirty-four SPVs including seven tankers, whilst Hessle's 102 craft included eleven tugs, two of which were the first of several ship-towing craft for Cory, thirty-six lighters/dumb barges, eighteen self-propelled tankers and, innovatively, nineteen trawlers (Thorne also built 4 in this decade). Both barge/lighter tugs and ship-handling tugs are included in the tug totals. Several of Thorne's newbuildings were completed at Hessle.

The 1950s also saw Dunstons' peak in the number of inland waterway craft produced for a whole variety of customers from earlier years, such as Hargreaves, Hodgsons, Furleys, Cooks, River Lighterage Co, Union Lighterage Co, Thames Steam Tug & Lighterage Co, Corys, General Lighterage Co and APCM. New customers came along, including the D&IWE (later BTC and eventually BWB), London & Rochester Trading Co, Whitakers, Flixborough Shipping, the Port of London Authority, Esso, Vectis Shipping and Humphrey & Grey (Lighterage). BOCM, successors to Selby Oil Mills, also resumed their pre-1922 links with Dunstons by ordering two dumb barges and a fleet of eighteen SPV's, constructed at Thorne between 1953 and 1962.

T.770 *(06-03-50)* Jondor *(116ft x 17½ft x 8ft), one of three motor tank barges of 250 tons capacity, fitted with a 150bhp Crossley diesel engine, built for John H Whitaker of Hull and shown on trials when new. Eventually, Whitakers became operators of the largest fleet of tanker barges on the Humber.*

Jondor *coming light down the Ouse in 1978 after delivering fuel oil to York glassworks.*

S.629 *(28-03-50)* Bonnybridge *(126ft x 25ft x $13\frac{1}{2}$ ft), Dunstons' first trawler, a single screw vessel, was built for the Great Western Fishing Co of Aberdeen and powered by a 565bhp Mirrlees diesel engine.*

S.658 *(31-03-50)* St.Luke *(84ft x 21½ ft x 10ft), Dunstons' first all-welded trawler. The vessel was powered by a 270bhp Mirrlees engine, built for St Andrew's Fishing Co, and registered at Lowestoft.*

S.665 *(14-07-50) Floating Dock (134ft x 33ft x 6ft). under construction at Hessle.*

The Floating Dock shortly after being launched at Hessle. The apparatus was constructed for the APCM so that they could maintain their own tugs and barges on the Thames.

S.665

FLOATING DOCKING PONTOON

Dimensions: Length 134' 0"
Breadth 33' 0"
Depth 6' 0"

This is a simple and economical way of maintaining barges in tidal waters. Firstly the dock is floated at high tide above a prepared level sea bed, as the tide recedes the dock is left high and dry on this surface and the sea cocks are opened. As the tide rises the dock is flooded and remains underwater and a barge is then floated into position above the dock. As the tide falls the barge is left inside the dock resting on seating blocks and the sea cocks are then shut. Thus the barge is left clear of the water no matter what state the tide is in. The procedure is reversed when the barge is fully repaired and maintainenced.

Owners: Associated Portland Cement Manufacturers.

Built by:
Richard Dunston (Hessle) Ltd.,
Haven Shipyard,
Hessle,
Yorkshire,
England.

Details of the Floating Dock as described in Dunstons' Album.

T.783-5 *(July/Aug 1950) an unnamed cargo and Passenger Lighter (102½ ft x 26ft x 6ft), built for 'Crown Agents for the Colonies' and shown on an East African river, having been dismantled after building before being shipped out.*

A postcard view of Hessle Haven in the early 1950s with S.661 *(16-11-50)* Somme *(152½ft x 25ft x 12ft), a single-screw, 465hp British Polar-engined diesel coaster built for W H Muller being completed outside Dunstons' yard.*

T.798 *(13-12-50)* Flanagan *(80ft x 20ft x 9½ft), a 'diesel Thames lighter' fitted with a 66bhp Kelvin engine built for the London & Rochester Trading Co (Crescent Shipping) at work in one of the London docks. The Company also had four lighters, 2 towing launches and two more SPVs built by Dunstons.*

T.802 *(19-05-52)* Recruit *(73ft x 19½ft x 19½ft x 10½ft), a single screw diesel tug, fitted with a 670bhp Crossley engine, built for Wm.Cory & Son, seen at work on the Thames with Dunston-built lighters.*

The tug Recruit, *still owned by Cory, passing down the Thames beneath Westminster bridge with containerised refuse barges in tow during 2001, by which date a 1196bhp replacement engine had been fitted.*

S.670 *(26-05-52)* Esso Abingdon *(160ft x 32ft x 11ft) one of fifteen diesel tankers built at Hessle in the 1950s for Esso Transportation. The vessel was fitted with a 400bhp engine and made many voyages beneath London's bridges bringing petrol from Essex refineries to upriver depots in the Fulham area.*

T.793/4 *(Oct/Dec 1952)* R.A.Leigh *(93ft x 21½ ft x 10½ ft). one of two 'twin screw steam tugs' built for South African Railways, each fitted with two 250ihp McKie & Baxter engines. These were the final steam powered craft to be built by Dunstons.*

T.836 *(18-12-52)* Milligan *(85ft x 20ft x 9½ft), a 'welded diesel lighter', named, like Flanagan on page xx, after a comedian, with a 66bhp Kelvin engine, built for the London & Rochester Trading Co. heads down Bow Creek in 1956 loaded with gasworks coke for a cement company on the Medway.*

T.838 *(23-05-53)* Plastron *(70ft x 20½ ft x 9½ ft), a diesel ship-handling tug powered by a 440bhp Crossley engine, was built for the Port of London Authority (PLA) and is shown when new acting as stern tug to the* Dominion Monarch *in King George V Dock.*

T.848 *(09-05-53)* William H.Gant *(81½ft x 14½ft x 7ft), one of three 'welded dumb 150-ton capacity dry cargo barges' built for the Nottingham-based Trent Carriers. under tow on the river Humber in the 1960s.* Jack Radford

T.847 *(21-05-53)* Swiftstone *(73ft x 19½ft x 10½ft) another diesel tug with a 670bhp Crossley engine built for Corys, photographed from Tower Bridge in 1989 as it heads upriver past the Royal Yacht* Britannia *with barges going to collect containerised refuse.*

T.850 *(30-05-53)* Leicester Trader *(81½ft x 14½ft x 7ft), a sister vessel to* William H Gant *(see page 74), built for Trent Carriers, transhipping a cargo in Goole's Barge Dock in the 1950s.*

Norman Burnitt

T.851 *(26-10-53)* Regality *(117½ft x 17½ft x 8ft), was built for Whitakers along with T.852* Regina E, *as sister 'welded power tank barge' to* Jondor *(see page 65) and fitted with a 150bhp Crossley engine. The vessel is shown being launched.*

T.852 *(21-12-53)* Regina E *(118ft x 17½ft x 8ft). This montage of pictures was taken in 1971 at a river Hull dry dock as the tanker, fitted with a 180bhp replacement Lister Blackstone engine was being lengthened by 17½ ft to increase its carrying capacity.* Jack Radford

T.855 *(01-12-53)* Ellen Elizabeth *(61ft x 15½ft x 7½ft), one of six barges built for Flixborough Shipping Co. and one of only two (T.853* Enid Hilda *was the other) fitted with engines (40bhp Listers) when built, due to the company's lack of funds. The others were engined later, having been towed by the powered craft in the meantime. The vessel is shown on Stanley Ferry aqueduct in 1957.*
Arthur Watts

T.859 *(17-04-53)* BW No.4 *(82ft x 14´ft x 7ft) built for the D&IWE as 'a steel pontoon for grab crane', here, renamed* Calder, *with its 1961-fitted crane and a 120bhp 6-cylinder Ford engine, is shown bringing steel reinforcing beams to Gowdall railway bridge over the river Aire, which was inaccessible by road.* T.111 *(24-04-23)* Enterprise *(56½ft x 14½ft x 5ft), a workboat built for the S&SYNC to be towed by horse but now with a 40bhp Lister engine installed, has been fitted with two scissor jacks supporting working platforms for placing beneath the bridge. Both craft were owned by Alan Oliver (Workboats) at the time of this 2002 photograph.*

T.873 *(09-09-53)* Selby Phillipa *(97ft x 17½ ft x 7½ ft) was the first of eighteen SPVs built by Dunstons for BOCM when they decided to replace their tug-hauled fleet of dumb barges with motor vessels. The barge, fitted with a 62bhp Lister engine, is shown together with the twelfth vessel to join the fleet,* T.956 Selby Janet, *moored at BOCM's wharf on the Ouse at Barlby, near Selby, in 1979.*

Two other members of the Selby SPV fleet, T.874 Selby Corrie *and* T.924 Selby Peter, *are shown on page 16 flanking* Selby Argo.

T.876 *(16-02-54)* Kappa *(72ft x 15½ ft x 8ft), a 'single screw diesel barge' launched at the same time as sister ship* T.875 Theta *and built for the D&IWE. Fitted with a 48bhp Gardner engine, the vessel is shown discharging a cargo at Leeds Terminus on the A&CN in the mid-1950s.*

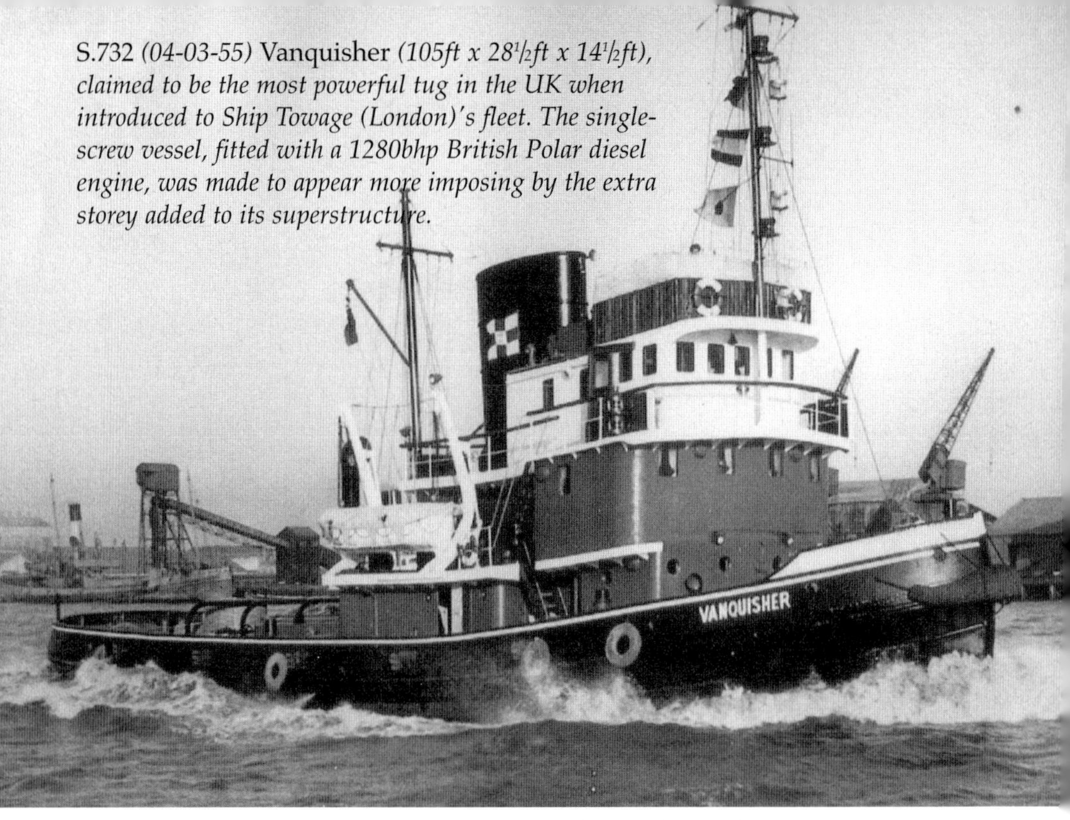

S.732 *(04-03-55)* Vanquisher *(105ft x 28½ft x 14½ft), claimed to be the most powerful tug in the UK when introduced to Ship Towage (London)'s fleet. The single-screw vessel, fitted with a 1280bhp British Polar diesel engine, was made to appear more imposing by the extra storey added to its superstructure.*

T.914 *(18-06-56)* Esso Leeds *(123ft x 17½ft x 8ft), one of three diesel tank barges fitted with a 180bhp Lister Blackstone engine driving through a 360 degree rotateable propulsion unit instead of a rudder, built for Esso Petroleum for use on the Humber waterways. The vessel is seen making a token appearance on the S&SYN (where it never worked) at the opening of a new lock at Long Sandall in 1959.*

Esso Leeds *at work on the A&CN, leaving Ferrybridge flood lock bound for Leeds with a cargo of petrol loaded on the Humber at Saltend, near Hull.*

T.934 *(30-10-56)* Sunweld *(86ft x 21ft x 8½ft) was one of six 200 ton plus capacity hatched swim barges [a swim barge's bow and stern slope markedly from the deck at both its forepeak and aftpeak down to the bottom of the vessel. In this case, the fore 'overhang' thus created was 17ft, whilst that at the stern was 15½ft]. The craft were built in 1956 for the London & Rochester Trading Co. and* Sunweld *is featured on the front cover of one of Dunstons' brochures.*

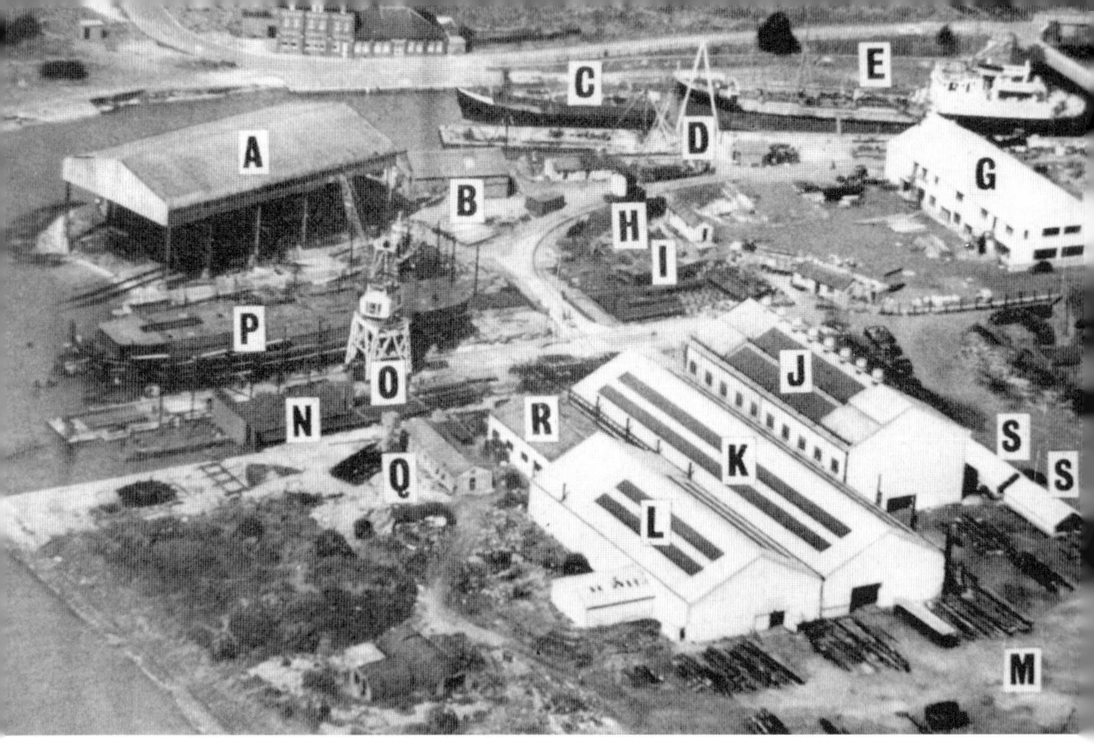

An aerial view of the Hessle site looking west in late 1957. C is S.749, the trawler Bahamas *and D is the tanker* S.738, Stansted, *both at fitting out berths; at P and N the tank ships S.751* Esso Woolston *and* S.752 Esso Lyndhurst *are under construction, A is a covered berth, the shipwrights', joiners', electricians', blacksmiths' and painters' shops are at G, J is the welding shop, K and L hold the platers' shops and M is the steel storage area.*

The welding shop at Hessle is shown with prefabricated parts being prepared for assembly. The unit nearest the camera is inverted for ease of welding. This same procedure was also practised at Thorne. Frank Dallas Collection

T.957 *(28-06-57)* Topsy *(80ft x 16½ ft x 8ft) was one of several dumb lighters built for Hargreaves in the 1950s to serve Ferrybridge 'A' and 'B' power stations. This vessel and another new sister vessel are shown being towed away from 'A' station by the towing barge* T.382 (16-03-42) Lawson *(60ft x 14½ft x 6½ft) after the barge naming ceremony. All the 200-ton capacity lighters had been motorised with 48bhp engines by the mid-1960s.*

T.958 *(20-02-58)* Joyce *(80ft x 16½ ft x 8ft), sister to* Topsy, *crossing Stanley ferry aqueduct in 1979, when motorised, with a cargo of coal for Ferrybridge 'B' loaded at Parkhill Colliery.*

T.966 *(16-10-57)* Gladys Lillian *(111ft x 17½ ft x 7½ ft) one of a pair of 'all-welded motor lighters' powered by 94bhp Ruston & Hornsby engines built for the BTC, as the operators of British nationalised waterways were then termed. The vessel is shown in the early 1970s, lengthened to 140ft and loaded with a cargo from Knostrop depot, coming down the Leeds branch of the A&CN past Astley Staithe.*

T.988 *(20-01-58) launched as* Bernard C.Wallace *but renamed* The President *(41ft x 14½ ft x 9ft), was a diesel tug built for Leeds Industrial Co-operative Society to tow their dumb craft from A&CN coal-loading staithes to their Leeds depot at Victoria wharf. Moored on the inside of the tug at this wharf are some of the Society's fleet of dumb barges, including* T.212 *(28-09-37)* R.Marshall *(61½ ft x 15ft x 6½ ft).* S.375 *(13-05-36)* Albion *(60ft x 14½ ft x 6½ ft), their towing barge, is also visible to the left of this 1960s view.*
Yorkshire Waterways Museum, Goole

Chapter Five

The 1960s

IN 1960, A NEW DEEP WATER JETTY protruding out into the Humber was constructed at Hessle so that new buildings could remain afloat whilst being fitted out. Previously, craft were moored in the tidal Hessle Haven, which almost dried out at low water. Also, in 1961, the Hessle yard finally began to use the name of its owner when it became Richard Dunston (Hessle)Ltd.

Welding finally completely replaced riveting as the means of joining plates together in the mid-1960s. Dunstons' first tractor tugs, whereby the propelling units are situated amidships rather than at the stern, appeared in mid-decade.

Of the 229 craft built at Thorne in the 1960s, fifty-three were diesel tugs (including nine push tugs), 118 were dumb barges/lighters, thirty-nine

T.999 *(27-09-60)* James Jones *(96½ft x 17½ft x 7½ft), a diesel lighter fitted with a 94bhp engine, was built for the long-established Goole-based carrier G D Holmes and is shown penning into Goole docks from the Ouse along with the workboat* Thomas H *(see also page 44) in the mid-1970s after a replacement 150hp engine had been installed.*

were motor barges and eight were trawlers. The nine push tugs and thirty-five of the dumb barges were to be used in delivering coal to the new Ferrybridge 'C' power station on the A&CN. Another major contract involving the A&CN in the decade was for fourteen SPVs to supply Skelton Grange power station, near Leeds. Mention should also be made of the eight tugs and twelve barges built to the order of Gray, MacKenzie & Co. for work in the Arabian Gulf.

At Hessle, 101 craft were built, fifty-three were diesel tugs, ninteen were dumb barges/lighters, ten were SPVs (all of which were tankers and included two 275ft x 42ft x 14ft craft for the Hull Gates Shipping Co.) and fifteen were trawlers. Again, several Thorne-built craft were completed at Hessle and the first *Hessle Flyer* was built at Thorne to transport parts to Hessle.

By the end of a decade which, in 1963, saw 13 million tons lightered annually on the Thames using 4,600 lighters hauled by 215 tugs, more than sixty tugs and well over 400 lighters had been contributed to the scene by Dunstons. Unfortunately however, throughout the 1960s, Thames lighterage was in severe decline and very few new craft were built for this after the end of the decade.

T.1039 *(30-05-60)* Brodsworth *(41ft x 14½ft x 9ft) was one of three diesel tugs (*T.987 West Riding *and* T.1040, Kellingley *were the others) built for BTC's Compartment Boat (Tom Pudding) fleet (out of a total of seven) when the fleet's steam tugs were being replaced. They were fitted with 135bhp Lister Blackstone engines.* Brodsworth *is shown drawing the first half of a loaded Goole-bound train out of the New Junction Canal's Sykehouse lock in 1978.*

T.1040 *(02-09-60)* Kellingley *(41ft x 14½ft x 9ft), another one of the three Dunston-built Pudding tugs, is shown on the S&SYN shortly after leaving Doncaster with a train of loaded pans.*

T.1056, *(no date given, but registered at Hull in 1961)* Hessle Flyer *(110ft x 21ft x 9ft), built to transport parts between Dunstons' Thorne and Hessle sites because so much fitting out of Thorne-built craft was undertaken at Hessle. The vessel, fitted with a 115bhp Deutz engine, was sold to G.D.Holmes and renamed* Maureen Anne W *in 1963. It is shown prior to being relaunched with its new name at Hessle.*

Maureen Anne W *in 1983, after being acquired by Gainsborough Shipping, passing beneath Keadby Bridge on the River Trent, loaded with a cargo for its owners' wharf at Beckingham.*

S.782 *(01-12-61)* Carnaby *(87½ft x 39ft x 14ft), a pontoon built for Simon Handling Engineers to be converted into a floating elevator lies moored at Hull.*

Carnaby *at work in 1962 after completion, transhipping grain from ship to inland waterway craft in King George Dock, Hull.*
Hull Maritime Museum

No 143. A&CN OS 1556 and No 144, A&CN OS 1158]
T.1082 *(02-04-62)* No 15 *(83½ft x 17ft x 8ft), a 200 ton capacity diesel coal barge fitted with a 62bhp Lister engine, was the final one of fourteen built for Cawoods Wharton in the six months between November 1961 and April 1962 to service the new power station at Skelton Grange, Leeds. The vessel is shown in the late 1960s, (above) heading along the A&CN shortly after loading at Parkhill Colliery on the Wakefield Arm and below partially discharged at the power station wharf.*
Andy Horn Collection and Jarvis Whitton

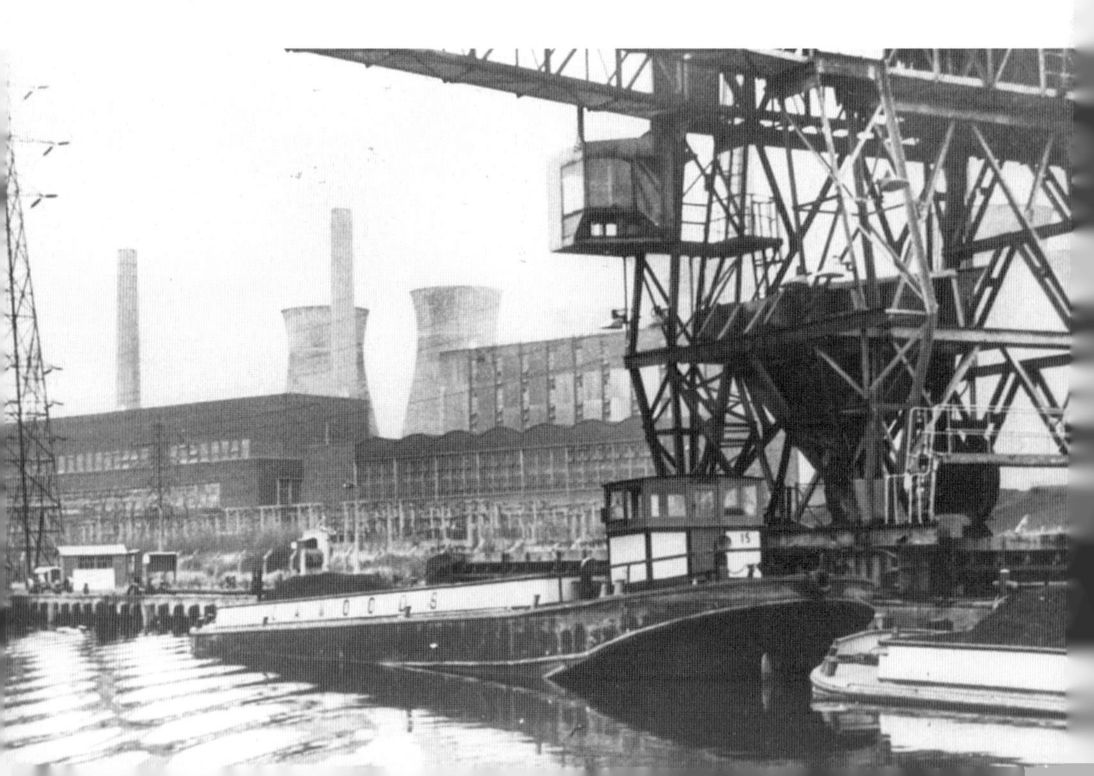

T.1091 *(23-03-62)* Recourse *(69ft x 18½ ft x 9ft), a diesel tug built for Gray, MacKenzie & Co being hoisted aboard* M V Nigarstan *for carriage to the Arabian Gulf.*

Recourse *and sister tug* T.1092 *(23-03-62)* Rencounter *loaded aboard* Nigarstan.

T.1112 *(23-07-62)* Murius *(90ft x 20ft x 8ft), a twin-screw diesel lighter powered by two 66bhp Kelvin engines, built for Vectis Shipping Co. is shown at work in Southampton docks in 1993 when owned by Williams Shipping.*

T.1116 *(19-10-62)* Selby Maurice *(98ft x 19ft x 8ft), the final diesel lighter of the eighteen built for BOCM as they changed from tug-hauled dumb craft to SPVs. Yet to be fitted with a 110bhp Gardner, the vessel is shown on launch day at*

Several members of the Selby fleet of SPVs (loaded) and some of the older dumb barges they were still using (light) are shown in King George Dock, Hull as a huge cargo of shea nuts that had been shipped in was being transhipped to barge in 1980.

S.798 Diction *(96ft x 23ft x 9½ ft), a diesel lighter built for The London and Rochester Trading Co. powered by a 182bhp Kelvin engine and seen here in Cornwall loading calcified seaweed on Truro's river in 1986 when owned by J Darling (Import & Export) Services.*

An aerial view of Hessle yard looking east, showing the 1960-constructed jetty into the Humber.

David Marley *(170ft x 36ft x 16½ft), a diesel hopper barge designed for dumping colliery waste at sea from the River Tyne. Built for Stephenson Clarke and shown on acceptance trials, the vessel was powered by a 980bhp British Polar engine.*

T.1154 *(no date given but registered at Hull in 1964)* Hessle Flyer II *(90ft x 20ft x 8ft), a successor to the larger and less manoeuvrable original* Hessle Flyer, *now sold to G D Holmes and trading as* Maureen Anne W *(see page 87), was fitted with a 67bhp English Electric motor driving through a Harbormaster outboard propulsion unit rather than its earlier mamesake's tiller and propeller. The vessel is shown on the canal at Thorne, leaving for Hessle with parts for fitting out of a vessel. On rare occasions it also delivered parts to Goole for craft being fitted out there.*

T.1165 *(02-10-65)* General VIII *(74ft x 20ft x 10ft), a 665bhp diesel tug built for Thames & General Lighterage, still at work on the Thames in 1983, though now with a 1196bhp engine, as it pulls loaded refuse barges beneath Hungerford Bridge, after transfer to Cory ownership. This was the final Thames lighterage tug to be built by Dunstons. At the time of this photograph, annual lighter cargoes had fallen to 1.75 million tons, carried in only 900 lighters pulled by forty-five tugs (These figures may be compared with those for 1963 quoted on page 86).*

S.802 *(19-03-66)* Sir Winston Churchill *(103ft x 25ft), a topsail three-masted schooner built for the Sail Training Association with accommodation for 36 trainees and fitted with two 120bhp auxiliary Perkins engines, is shown at Falmouth in late 1966.*

A tug and two lighters heading up Bow Creek from the Thames in the 1980s. BWB

S.838 *(18-08-66)* Leeside *($87\frac{1}{2}$ ft x 18ft x $6\frac{1}{2}$ ft), a 180 ton capacity dumb lighter built for Vokins, was one of the final Thames lighters produced by Dunstons. Carrying imported bales of copper sheet eleven miles upriver to Enfield Rolling Mills at Brimsdown in 1983, the vessel has been drawn into one of the River Lea's Bow Locks, using an electric capstan and is about to be ejected using the same apparatus after rising. Sister vessel* S.840 Levity *(31-10-66) waits below the lock.*

A busy scene at Bow locks in the 1970s as a lighter bound downriver is hauled out of Bow locks by a tug, with other lighters waiting to be penned through, both above and below the locks. BWB

T.1168 *(26-05-66))* CH 102 *(29ft x 14ft x 5ft), a pusher tug, was the second of nine to be built for Cawoods Hargreaves, each fitted with a 150bhp deck-mounted Dorman engine driving through a Harbormaster unit. They were designed to service the new Ferrybridge 'C' power station with coal carried in thirty-five dumb barges, also built by Dunstons. The tug is shown at the A&CN's Astley staithe in the early 1970s as one of the pans is being loaded and another pan,* T.1181, *(05-05-66)* CH 14, *waits. Cawoods' motor barge* T.1075 *(08-01-62)* No 7 *is also waiting to load.* Jarvis Whitton

T.1218 *(11-09-67)* CH 106 *(29ft x 14ft x 5ft), another push tug built for Cawoods Hargreaves pushes the usual train of three $55\frac{1}{2}$ ft x 17ft x $9\frac{1}{2}$ ft pans carrying a total of over 500 tons of coal at 4-lane ends, Castleford, where the A&CN's Wakefield and Leeds arms meet to go along Castleford cut towards Ferrybridge power station in the early 1970s.* BWB

A train of three Cawoods Hargreaves' loaded pans is being pushed towards the channel leading to the tippler at Ferrybridge 'C' power station in 1987. Each pan is placed in turn benneath the hoist, lifted and its 170-ton cargo of coal tipped by turning it longitudinally through 135 degrees. the nine-minute cycle was completed by lowering the pan and pushing it out of the other end of the channel. With replacements of the tugs' engines and propulsion units, this traffic flourished until the end of 2002.

S.835 *(20-12-66)* Balla *(95ft x 26ft x 8ft), was one of a pair of tugs built for service with Pakistan River Steamers. Two 480bhp Crossley engines worked through Kort steering nozzles in a tunnel stern and the tugs were suitable for push, side-on or pull towing. The vessels travelled to Pakistan under their own power.* Hull Maritime Museum

The Hull Mutual Insurance Co's fleet of Dunston-built tugs photographed in Hull's St Andrew's (fish) Dock in the late 1960s; T.1202 *(12-01-67)* Neptune, T.1152 *(26-11-64)* Triton, T.1153 *(07-11-64)* Zephyr *and* T.1113 *(28-03-63)* Aurora *(all 55ft x 17ft x 8½ft), described as* Voith Schneider *Water Tractors and fitted with 350hp Mirrlees engines. Also visible is the TID tug* T.495 *(28-07-44)* Bernie *(ex-*TID 86*).* Triton *and* Zephyr *moved to a Thames-based company and* Neptune *to Milford Haven in 1980.*

A Voith-Schneider *propulsion unit which rotated on a vertical axis and was used as a substitute for a traditional propeller.* Hull Maritime Museum

T.1207 *(21-02-67)* Theraputtabhaya *(85ft x 17ft x 8ft), a single screw diesel tug powered by a 380bhp Crossley engine, was built for the Colombo Port Authority of Sri Lanka and intended for the towage of barges.*

S.850 *(06-12-67)* Humber Guardian *(150ft x 33ft x 16ft), a twin screw buoy-handling vessel powered by two 625bhp Polar engines, was designed and built by Dunstons for the Humber Conservancy Board and is shown in use by them.*
Hull Maritime Museum

S.853 *(24-01-68)* M.S.C.Buffalo *(87ft x 28½ ft x 8ft), a craneboat for the Manchester Ship Canal Co shown here on the Canal near Runcorn in 1991.*

T.1241 *(31-01-68)* M.S.C. Traverse *(30ft x 12ft x 5ft), a ferry propelled by jets of water built for the Manchester Ship Canal Company in use on that waterway, at Irlam, near Warrington, when new.* Hull Maritime Museum

T.1231 *(29-02-68)* Speedwell *(56ft x 16ft x 8ft), a single screw diesel tug powered by a 330bhp engine, was built for BWB. The vessel is shown in 1978 scouring the river Severn channel between Tewkesbury and Gloucester.*

S.862 *(23-10-68)* Bouncer *(110ft x 24ft x 9ft), one of four diesel tankers built in the 1960s for G T Stratford & Sons powered by a 240bhp Kelvin engine. The vessel vas pictured from Tower Bridge, heading up the Thames with a cargo for Fulham in 1983, when operated by Bowker & King.*

S.863 *(27-06-69)* Bisley *(202ft x 30ft x 14½ ft), a diesel-powered tanker barge built for Bowker & King, fitted with a 600bhp Lister Blackstone main engine, used mainly to deliver petroleum liquids from Severn estuary terminals to depots such as Quedgeley on the Gloucester & Sharpness Canal. The vessel is shown entering Sharpness docks whilst returning light from Quedgeley in 1981.*

T.1258/9 *(16-05-69)* GM.24/GM.25 *(125ft x 26ft x 8½ ft), two 500 ton capacity, double-hatched barges built for Gray, MacKenzie & Co, one of which, together with other GM craft, including the tug* T.1253 *(12-05-69)* Rasheed *(69ft x 19½ft x 9ft), is shown as deck cargo aboard a ship bound for the Arabian Gulf.* Hull Maritime Museum

Chapter Six

1970-2009

DUNSTONS ENHANCED their reputation for tug-building after the Second World War. In addition to traditional diesel screw tugs, they had built totals of sixty-three Kort nozzle/Kort rudder tugs before the end of the 1970s (forty-six at Hessle, seventeen at Thorne), thirty-one tugs with *Voith-Schneider* drive units (eleven at Hessle and twenty at Thorne) and were continuing with other innovative propulsion features.

In 1974, Dunstons became part of the Ingram Corporation and, in late 1986 they moved to the Dutch Damen Group.

Of the 157 craft built at Thorne during this period, before shipbuilding ceased in December 1984, fifty were ordered by the Ministry of Defence. The MoD also requisitioned thirty-two of the 144 vessels built at Hessle before that yard closed in 1994. Hessle also produced a few large ships

T.1270 *(06-03-70)* CH 32 *(55½ft x 17ft x 9½ft), one of the final batch of dumb barges built for Cawoods Hargreaves designed to be pushed to Ferrybridge 'C' power station, is the leading vessel of three shown entering Mexborough top lock in 1993, loaded with coal from Rotherham. By this time, 238bhp Volvo engines and Sykes' Hydromatic propulsion units had been installed on the tugs.*

(including dry cargo vessels and tankers, examples of these are given in this chapter), sixty-eight tugs were built there in this period, including fifteen more for the Alexandra Towing Company who were already using the six that had been built for them in the 1960s. The Hessle yard closed in 1994 as Dunston Ship Repairs were becoming established in Hull's William Wright Dock.

The final vessel built at Thorne was a steel COB boat *CB12* for BWB, completed 13-10-84 and, fittingly, a tug, the twin-screw *Annelies*, built for Damen, Dunstons' owners, was Hessle's last newbuilding, though hulls for two fishing vessels to be completed elsewhere followed later in 1994, and H.1011, *Weligouwa*, a suction dredger for the Sri Lankan government, was launched from the yard in April 1995 and finished off in Hull's William Wright Dock.

S.877 *(04-05-71)* Security *(260ft x 41½ft x 20½ft), was one of two sister ships built for F.T.Everard & Sons powered by two Newbery diesel engines, each of 900bhp.* Hull Maritime Museum

One of the inland waterway activities of the Ingram Corporation, which took over Dunstons in 1974, was the ownership and operation of craft in the USA. One of their tugs is shown pushing barges on the Mississippi river.

H.894 *(the first Hessle-built vessel with H. as prefix to its yard number) (14-04-76)* Kolla *(189ft x 37ft x 18½ft), one of three 1000 ton Tuna Clippers for Peruvian owners in Lima, the furthest base away from the UK that a newbuilding was ever ordered from Dunstons. The vessel was powered by a 3520bhp Ruston engine. The other two sister ships were supplied in kit form for assembly and completion at a Peruvian yard.*

H.913 *(08-12-77)* Wallasey *(95ft x 30ft x 16½ft) one of an eventual twenty-one ship-handling tugs built by Dunstons for the Alexandra Towing Co, was powered by a 2640bhp Ruston main engine and is seen, after delivery to its owners, heading up the Mersey past Liverpool's Pierhead.*

Wallasey *was a single-screw stern drive tug, driving through a variable pitch propeller within a Kort steering nozzle, clearly visible as the vessel is under construction at Hessle.* Hull Maritime Museum

T.1363 *(April 1980)* No 89615 Burnley *(57ft x 13ft x 3½ ft), one of a pair of maintenance barges built for BWB, each powered by a 44bhp Lister engine, is pictured on trials at Thorne.* Norman Burnitt

H.933 *(11-10-82)* Oilman *(203½ ft x 37ft x 16ft), one of three single screw coastal tankers designed and built by Dunstons for Rowbotham Tankships to carry 2028 cubic metres (71,622 cu.ft) of cargo. The vessel was fitted with a 1700bhp Ruston main engine and is shown on acceptance trials on the Humber.* Hull Maritime Museum

T.1372 *(Jan 1983)* Milford *(75ft x 21ft x 10ft), built for the MoD as an 'A' type Fleet Tender, is shown being launched at Thorne.* Frank Dallas Collection

H.942 *(27-11-83)* Koluama *(129½ ft x 26ft x 5½ ft) a ramped tanker barge to transport oil fuel and building materials, was built for the Coutinho Caro Co. to be used on a rural electrification scheme in Nigeria. The vessel was powered by two 84bhp Deutz engines, each flexibly coupled to a deck-mounted steerable propulsion unit. Two other vessels, ramped tanker barges,* T.1378/9 Segbama *and* Apoi, *were built at Thorne for work on the project.*
Hull Maritime Museum

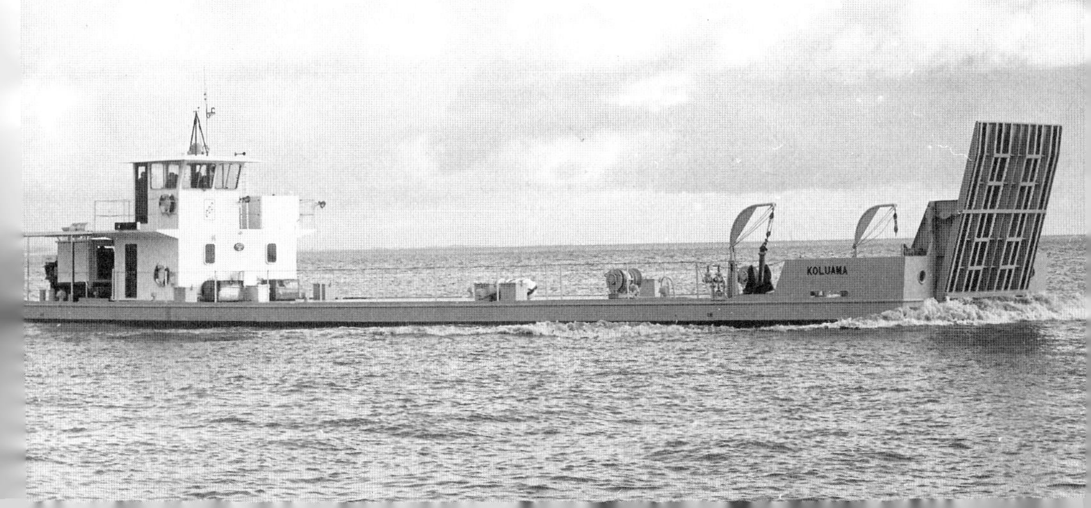

H.950 *(29-03-85)* Eston Cross *(88ft x 29ft x 11ft) a twin-screw tractor tug (see page 9) built for the Tees Towing Co. of Middlesbrough. Power from twin 1700bhp Ruston diesel engines is delivered to two Aquamaster propeller units fitted with Kort nozzles that are able to be rotated through 360 degrees about a vertical axis, the starboard one of which may be seen on this pre-launch picture. The Voith-Schneider units in the Hull Mutual fleet of tugs (shown on page 103) would be placed in similar positions to these Aquamaster units.*

H.951 *(12-02-86)* Flying Spindrift *(89½ ft x 29½ ft x 13ft), a stern-driven twin screw tug, was built for the Clyde Shipping Co of Glasgow. Two 1550bhp Ruston engines are used to power the twin Aquamaster units visible. Each unit is rotatable about a vertical axis and features a fixed-bladed propeller fitted with Kort nozzle.*

Hessle yard was taken over by Damen Shipyards, a Netherlands-based company owning nearly twenty other European yards, in November 1986. Dunstons' publicity never seemed to mention this fact, and this aerial view of Damen's Rotterdam yards from one of Dunstons' publications was described by them as 'modern repair facilities for vessels up to 25,000 tonnes deadweight offered through our European connections'.
Hull Maritime Museum

H.954 *(09-10-86)* Loch Riddon *(99ft x 33ft x 8½ft), one of four roll on/roll off car and passenger ferries, was designed and built for Caledonian MacBrayne to provide a year round service to Scottish West Coast Islands. Each vessel was powered by two Volvo Penta 330bhp engines.* Hull Maritime Museum

H.957 *(29-05-87)* MAC 1021 *(103½ft x 29½ft x 8½ft), a dumb generator load testing barge built for the MoD, being towed away after launching at Hessle.* Hull Maritime Museum

H.991 *(August 1990)* Bromley Pearl *(315ft x 41ft x 14ft), a single screw low air draught coaster, was built for Bromley Shipping. Subcontracted to Dunstons by Cochrane Shipbuilders of Selby, along with* Union Saturn, *both powered by a MAN-B & W diesel engine, the vessel is seen collecting its first cargo in Hull's King George Dock. The ship was acquired by Union Transport in 1995 and renamed* Union Pearl. Hull Maritime Museum

H.999 *(March 1992)* Tarquin Mariner, *H.1000 (May 1992)* Sunny Fellow *and* H.1001 *(August 1992)* Gammagas, *all (295½ ft x 49ft x 25½ ft), single screw liquefied petroleum gas carriers, were the three largest ships to be built by Dunstons. The vessels each had cargo capacities of 4,400 cubic metres (155,392 cubic feet) in their two tanks. All three craft were produced for members of the Unigas Consortium, powered by M.A.K. 4500bhp main engines and fitted with bow thrusters.* Tarquin Mariner *amd* Sunny Fellow *are shown being fitted out in Hull's Alexandra Dock.* Hull Maritime Museum

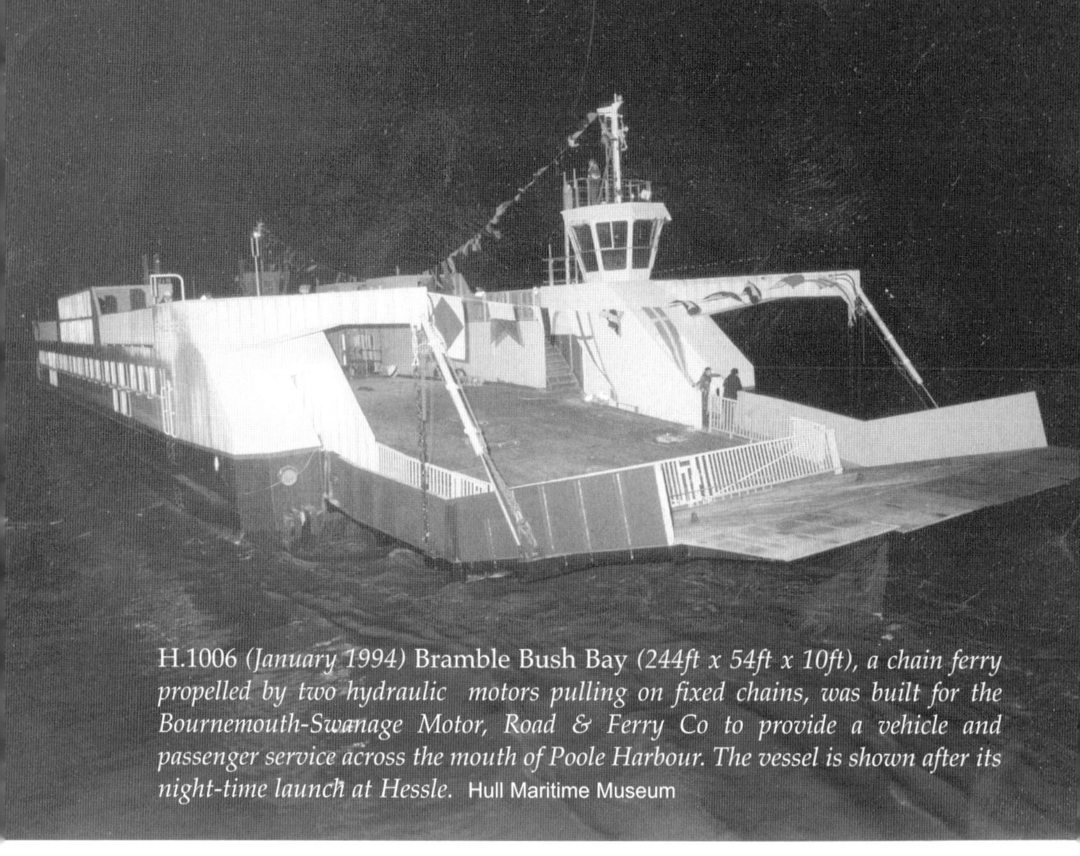

H.1006 *(January 1994)* Bramble Bush Bay *(244ft x 54ft x 10ft), a chain ferry propelled by two hydraulic motors pulling on fixed chains, was built for the Bournemouth-Swanage Motor, Road & Ferry Co to provide a vehicle and passenger service across the mouth of Poole Harbour. The vessel is shown after its night-time launch at Hessle.* Hull Maritime Museum

Bramble Bush Bay *in use leaving Sandbanks to cross to Shell Bay (for Swanage) in 2007.*

H.1007 *(April 1994)* Annelies *(131ft x 31ft x 16ft) a twin-screw tug built for Dunstons' then owners, Damen Trading and the last vessel to be built at Hessle before the yard closed. Fitting out was actually completed in one of the owners' yards in mainland Europe.* Hull Maritime Museum

The tanker barge Farndale H, *built by the Yorkshire Dry Dock Co. of Hull, was bought by Branford Barge Owners for conversion to a dry cargo vessel and this work is shown in progress during 2005 at Dunston Ship Repairs' premises in Hull's William Wright Dock. A new 400bhp Cummins diesel engine was fitted at the same time.*

Chapter Seven

Miscellany

THE FIRST NINE ILLUSTRATIONS relate to Henry Scarr's shipbuilding. Scarr moved from Beverley to Hessle in 1897 and that yard was taken over by Dunstons in 1932.

S.80 *(25-04-1896)* Southern Cross *a steel steam tug of 200ihp was built for the City Steam Towing Co by the Beverley-based shipbuilding partners, brothers Henry and Joseph Scarr, before the partnership was dissolved and Henry moved to Hessle. The tug was a founder member of the United Towing Co fleet in 1921.*
Hull Maritime Museum

A wooden sloop and small pleasure craft lie in Hessle yard around 1897 when Henry Scarr took over the yard. The yard then began building exclusively in iron and steel.

A Henry Scarr letterhead dating from the late nineteenth century, well before the company's Hessle yard was taken over by Dunstons.

HENRY SCARR LTD
National Telephones
No 85.
W. L. SCARR,
Beverley Road No 82.
IRON SHIPBUILDER AND REPAIRER
SLIPWAY FOR SHIPS UP TO 100 FEET.
ENGINEER &c.

S.164 *(22-02-06)* Kate *(65ft x 16ft x 7½ ft) a steel sloop, built for one of the Barracloughs, is shown flying its burgee on the Humber whilst competing in one of the annual Barton sloop regattas. These finished in 1929.* Hull Maritime Museum

S.123, *(23-03-01)* Pioneer *(98½ft x 18ft x 7½ft), a steel 'coasting steamer' built for J.H Wetherall & Co of Goole with a 125ihp Hedley & Boyd engine, was the first sea-going vessel to navigate inland to Leeds, where it arrived in August 1901. The vessel carried over 100 tons of China clay loaded at the Cornish port of Fowey and had a difficult voyage up the A&CN from Goole on a 7ft draft, where masts and funnel had to be lowered at almost every bridge encountered.*

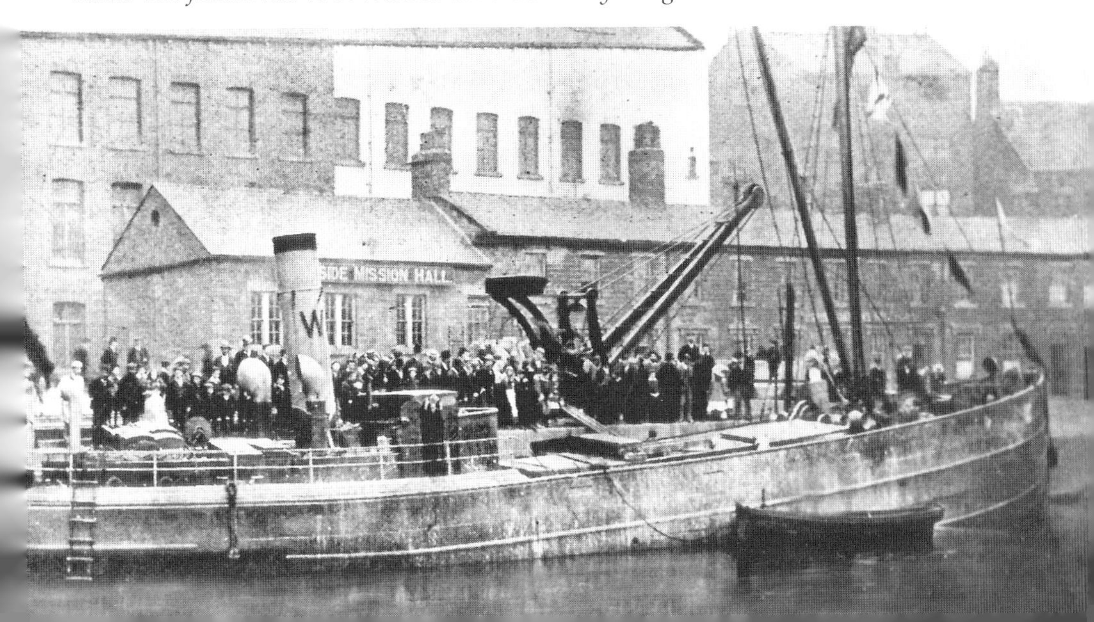

S.315 *(06-10-23)* Eleanor B *(61½ ft x 15½ ft x 7½ ft), built as a sailing keel for Jonas Braithwaite, was bought by Reckitt & Colman of Hull and motorised in 1946 with a 40bhp Atlantic engine. It is shown in 1955 bringing coal from Hatfield staithe on the S&SYN down the Trent to its owners' River Hull premises.*

The steam barge S.149 *(21-03-04)* Good Luck, *later renamed* Swiftsure *(60½ ft x 16½ ft x 7½ ft) and* S.322 *(24-03-25)* Motorman *(60½ ft x 40½ ft x 4½ ft), a twin screw diesel tug powered by two 72bhp Gardner engines, on stocks at Hessle yard in the late 1920s.* Hull Maritime Museum

S.313 *(25-10-23)* Ril Toto *(75ft x 20ft x 9ft), a lighter built for Spillers, being poled in Hull Harbour when new.*

Ril Toto *becoming the aft part of Waddingtons' large dumb barge* Confidence *at Swinton in early 1982. Its sister vessel* S.314 *(10-11-23)* Ril Dora *is lined up to become the fore part.*
BWB

Confidence *at work being push-towed, carrying a large German casting to Doncaster in late 1982. This was the first of four castings that it was designed to deliver from and return to Goole after machining.*

The Sheffield-size tanker barge Michael H *(see page 22) came over Rotherham weir in 1931 when a rope fouled its propeller and finished as shown against the river Don bridge. By this time, Harkers had added the suffix H to the names of members of their tanker fleet.*

In the 1950s Michael H *was converted into a dry cargo barge and is shown here in Goole's Ocean Lock (with the Sheffield-size* T.356 (16-12-40) Richard *alongside) en route from Hull to Rotherham carrying a cargo of grain.*
Humberside Libraries

The General Manager of the S&SYNC decreed that the collier Empire Laird *(see page 48) was too wide to be certain to pass safely through Keadby lock, its only exit to the sea (via the rivers Trent and Humber). If it had jammed in the lock, a large area around the village would be at risk of flooding with the high tide and the canal itself could have been drained at low water. Dunstons only option was to have a dam built above the lock to prevent these possible consequences. Construction of the dam above Keadby lock is shown in progress.*

Empire Laird *passing into Keadby lock.*

Empire Laird *successfully squeezing through Keadby lock and out into the River Trent.*

T. 539, *the oil-fired steam tug* OCO *(ex-TID 118), now owned by* BOCM, *sank at Swinefleet on the Yorkshire Ouse after being in collision with a coaster in 1961 and is shown prior to being raised.*

After raising and fitting of an enclosed wheelhouse, OCO *was renamed* Selby Olympia *and is shown in 1963 working off its owners' premises at Barlby.*

After the Second World War, many TID tugs were sold into tug fleets in Britain and abroad. T. 423, the coal-fired steam tug Tidspur *(ex-TID 23) was one of several that returned to the Humber and is shown working for the United Towing Co, hauling lighters out of Hull's Albert Dock sometime between 1956 and 1963.*

T.399, *the former coal-fired, steam-powered TID tug* Tarmo *(ex-*TID 1*) on a slip near Finland's Lappeenranta in the 1990s whilst still at work on the Saimaa canal and lakes after conversion to diesel power.* P.Sapila

T.504 *the oil-fired TID tug* Ernest Brown *(ex-*TID 95*) at work within sight of the Clifton Suspension bridge in Bristol Docks in the 1950s when owned by TR Brown & Sons.*

After purchase by Benjamin Perry & Sons of Bristol, T.415, *the coal-fired steam tug* TID 15 *was renamed* BP II. *This became* Salisbury *in 1965 when it was converted to diesel power with fitting of a 365bhp Ruston engine. The tug lies moored in Bristol's Cumberland basin.* Stephen Carter Collection

Salisbury *was purchased in 1980 by the Laxey Towing Co and is shown at work in Douglas harbour, Isle of Man in the mid-1980s.* Stephen Carter Collection

S.480, *the preserved Hessle-built, oil-fired, Ipswich-registered* TID 172, *away from its East Anglian base in 2004, as it makes an appearance at a steam rally in the Netherlands.* Chris Brown

The Humber Keel

The Humber Keel is the most historic of all British sailing ships being in direct descent from the Viking Longships which came raiding along the East Coast and up the Humber some fifteen hundred years ago.

Throughout the centuries the Humber Keels have kept the square-rig of the Longships traditional to the waterways of Yorkshire and North Lincolnshire.

Unfortunately today not one example of this historic craft remains trading under sail although a small fleet survived into the Second World War and one, the keel "Nar" of Hull, until 1949.

The Humber Keel Trust

The Humber Keel Trust was formed in December, 1952, to save the Humber Keel from complete extinction. It is now engaged in the restoration of the keel "Mayday."

It is the Trust's intention to put the keel "Mayday" into active commission, working under sail and earning her keep as far as possible. In addition it is hoped that during the summer months she will provide bona-fide sail training for the younger generation.

It is hoped also that the Lord Mayor of Kingston upon Hull, in his office of Admiral of the Humber, will, at least once a year, use the keel "Mayday" for a ceremonial sail.

The Keel "Mayday"

The keel "Mayday" was built at Thorne in 1900 by Messrs. Richard Dunston & Co. Ltd., for Messrs. Thomas Hanley & Co. Ltd., of Doncaster. Until 1941 she worked in the grain trade, carrying up to 106 tons of cargo from Hull to Doncaster.

In 1941 her mast, sails and leeboards, were removed and she was then towed as a dumb keel until 1951 when she was brought to Hull to work as a lighter.

On May 9th, 1953, the keel "Mayday" was presented to the Humber Keel Trust by Messrs. Joseph Rank Ltd.

Following a very extensive hull restoration the keel "Mayday" returned to service as a dumb keel in October, 1955. Since then she has carried a variety of cargoes including cattle cake, grain, coal, wire rods and palm kernels. She has visited Hull, Gainsborough, Selby, Doncaster and Wakefield.

The next step will be the complete restoration to sail and it is proposed to carry this out at an early date.

In 1963, the wooden Sheffield-size keel Mayday *(see page 13) was presented to the Humber Keel Trust who planned to restore the vessel and return it to sail, as indicated on these pages from one of their brochures. Sadly, this was unsuccessful and the* Mayday *was left to decay in Goole's timber pond where it is shown in 1968 (below).*

Loaded with paper at Hull and bound for Nottingham, the lighter William H Gant *(see page 74) and its towing barge jammed together as they were rising in the Trent's Stoke Bardolph lock. Draining the lock produced the problem shown with the craft even more firmly held together and a crane had to be brought to this rather remote site to offload the cargoes from both vessels, causing a twenty-four-hour delay on what was then a busy commercial route.*

Delivery of a sea-going vessel built at Thorne invariably involved passage down the Stainforth & Keadby Canal section of the S&SYN to Keadby where it passed through a lock and into the river Trent, from where it could reach the sea. The lock had dimensions of 79½ ft x 21½ ft, but longer vessels could be penned through when the Trent and canal 'made a level', near high water. Geoff Warnes photographed T.1049 *(28-06-61)* Silverfish *(93ft x 21½ ft x 10ft), a diesel trawler built for Huxley Fishing Co. as it passed from the yard, to the fitting out berth, down the canal and beyond. The vessel is first shown at its fitting-out berth just below Thorne railway bridge.*

As usual Dunstons hired two United Towing Company tugs to tow the completed vessel down the canal and through Keadby lock. Boatman *and* Waterman *are shown towing* Silverfish *in the early stages of the voyage.*
Geoff Warnes

The two tugs are shown mooring the trawler on arrival at Keadby. Geoff Warnes

Silverfish *refuelling after landing a catch at Lowestoft in summer 1962.*
Geoff Warnes

Built as a sloop in 1926, S.336 Soavita *(67½ ft x 16½ ft x 7½ ft) was purchased by G D Holmes in 1950, lengthened to 111½ ft and motorised with a 110bhp Gardner in 1955. It was then refurbished before being renamed* Vice Consul *at Harkers' Knottingley yard in 1963 where it is shown prior to its relaunching ceremony.*

Loaded with 200 tons of copper ore and bound from Hull to Gainsborough James Jones *(see page 85) collided with a coaster on the Trent and sank in 1979. The vessel is shown at Beckingham where a patch is being fitted over the large gash in its side.*

Gainsborough Shipping, the owners of James Jones, *sold the damaged barge to John Dean and he shortened the vessel to produce the push tug* Jamie, *shown leaving Leeds with a bunkering pontoon destined for Hull marina in 1983.*

Salvager A *(see page 23) was built as a sloop. It was lengthened in 1959 to 86½ ft and fitted with an 80hp Gardner engine. Whilst waiting to load palm kernels ex-ship in Goole's West Dock in 1982, it was run down and sunk by a German coaster. The photograph was taken almost immediately after the incident.*
Norman Burnitt

The full extent of the damage to Salvager *became evident after it had been raised and taken to a local boatyard. The vessel was then scrapped.*

T.863 *(01-10-52)* Snatchette *(41ft x 12ft x 6½ft), a 'Diesel Launch' was built for the London & Rochester Trading Co. for work on the Medway. In 1983, Acaster Water Transport bought the vessel and had it brought under its own power up the East Coast back to the Humber. Unfortunately, the Master Mariner navigating the tug turned inland too early, but after a couple of weeks being neaped at Gibraltar Point, near Skegness, it arrived at its destination and is shown shortly afterwards in a delapidated state on the A&CN at Rawcliffe Bridge, near Goole.*

After the fitting of an elevated wheelhouse and pusher 'knees' Snatchette *became the push tug* Little Shifta. *Later, a retractable hydraulic wheelhouse was fitted and the vessel is shown sporting this in Naburn lock, near York in 1994.*

Danum *(see page 25) eventually became a private residential vessel used mainly for cruising the French waterways and is shown out of the water at a boatyard in Arques, northern France, in the 1990s.* Robert and Jill Cowley

Hegaro (see page 46) was built for Hodgsons of Beverley but sold onto the Thames and shown there in use as a bookboat. Now the vessel is reported to have become a houseboat on the Medway at Rochester. Derek Grindell Collection

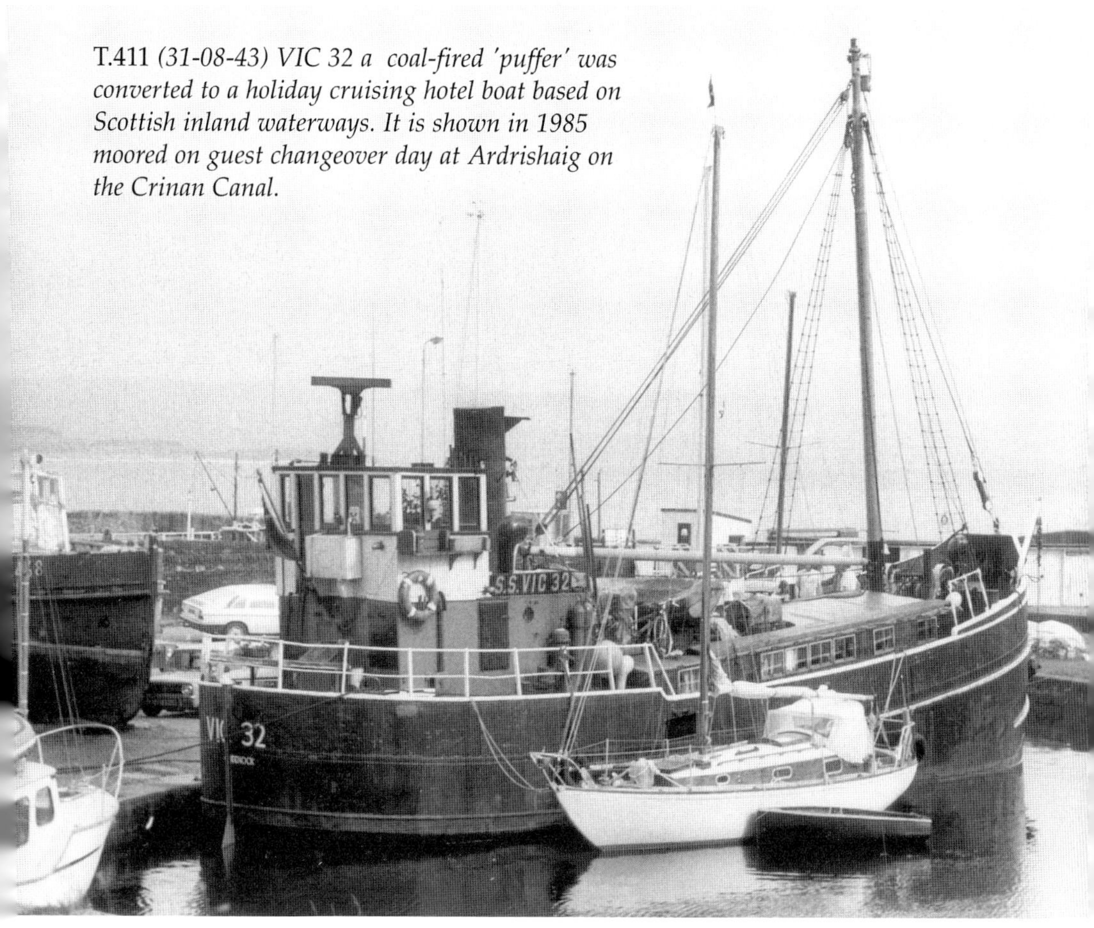

T.411 *(31-08-43) VIC 32 a coal-fired 'puffer' was converted to a holiday cruising hotel boat based on Scottish inland waterways. It is shown in 1985 moored on guest changeover day at Ardrishaig on the Crinan Canal.*

T.966 *(16-10-57) Hornshaw Water Transport's* Gladys Lillian *(see page 84) was built for the BTC, lengthened once from 111ft to 140ft and later lengthened again to 156ft, fitted with a bow section from another vessel and a reconditioned Gardner engine in 2006, before being renamed* Heather Rose H, *after the owner's daughter. Still carrying cargoes, it is shown on the Trent, near Besthorpe, loaded with aggregate for Whitwood on the A&CN in 2006.* John Noble

A candidate for the most unusual conversion of a Dunston-built vessel involved construction of a Chinese restaurant on Selby Virgo*, a sister ship of* Selby Argo *(**see page 16**), built at Thorne in 1921. Floating at its moorings in Brighton Marina, held by sturdy posts at bow and stern to enable it to rise and fall with water levels, the* Pagoda *was photographed in 2007.* John Hinchliffe

After Dunstons left Hessle, their site was used for a time to handle waterborne cargoes and, after discharging scrap iron there, Anke Bettina *is shown loading used Lada cars for delivery to eastern Europe where pollution controls were less stringent than they became in the UK.*

After Dunstons left Thorne, a private housing estate was built on the site of their boatyard with some roads named after Dunstans (sic) as shown.

ALSO AVAILABLE FROM WHARNCLIFFE'S
TRANSPORT THROUGH THE AGES SERIES

The River & Canal Sections of the Air & Calder Navigation
Mike Taylor, ISBN 1 903425379

The Forgotten Canals of Yorkshire
Wakefield to Swinton via Barnsley
Roger Glister, ISBN 1 903425387

Trams Around Dewsbury & Wakefield
Norman Ellis, ISBN 1 903425409

Trams & Trollybuses in Doncaster
Richard Buckley, ISBN 1 903425298

A Historical Dictionary of Railways in the British Isles
David Wragg, ISBN 9781844680474

INDEX OF CRAFT

William H Gant
Zephyr